60 0061818 X

TELEPEN

KU-490-007

RELIGION AND SOCIAL CONFLICT
IN SOUTH ASIA

INTERNATIONAL STUDIES
IN
SOCIOLOGY AND SOCIAL ANTHROPOLOGY

General Editor
K. ISHWARAN

VOLUME XXII

RELIGION AND SOCIAL
CONFLICT IN SOUTH ASIA

LEIDEN
E. J. BRILL
1976

RELIGION AND SOCIAL CONFLICT IN SOUTH ASIA

EDITED BY

BARDWELL L. SMITH

WITHDRAWN

LEIDEN
E. J. BRILL
1976

ISBN 90 04 04510 4

Copyright 1976 by E. J. Brill, Leiden, The Netherlands

All rights reserved. No part of this book may be reproduced or translated in any form, by print, photoprint, microfilm, microfiche or any other means without written permission from the publisher

PRINTED IN THE NETHERLANDS

CONTENTS

Religion, Social Conflict and the Problem of Identity in South Asia: An Interpretive Introduction

BARDWELL L. SMITH

Carleton College, Northfield, U.S.A.

A TITLE AS broad as *Religion and Social Conflict in South Asia* provides the licence to include all sorts of items under its umbrella. Yet it also incurs the responsibility of suggesting threads which link the several essays together and help to investigate more deeply religion's relationship to the social order, especially its role within social conflict. The single most recurring feature of this relationship examined here is the problem of personal and corporate identity, arising in a variety of forms as social structures (of which religion is always a component) encounter, stimulate and resist forces of change upon a continuously shifting modern scene. To explore this phenomenon essays were solicited from persons representing several disciplines and the decision made to limit the focus to a few situations within India, Bangladesh and Sri Lanka (Ceylon), where the problems of identity are both compounded and enriched by the spectrum of ethnic and religious groups present in each country.

Though the seven essays included here overlap in several ways, they may also be grouped in three categories, in some cases cutting across national lines. The first two, by B. G. Gokhale and Cyriac Pullapilly, examine the movements stimulated by B. R. Ambedkar, roughly between 1923 and 1956, on behalf of untouchables in India (especially among the Mahars) and by Sri Narayana Guru in the late nineteenth and early twentieth centuries among the low caste Izhavas of Kerala. The next three chapters deal, among other things, with opportunities and problems caused by decisive constitutional and legal changes occurring with India, Bangladesh and Sri Lanka which gave the promise of new social status to groups previously discriminated against without being able to deliver these changes automatically. The final two essays focus principally on tensions observable within Ceylon, though not absent elsewhere, between different income and caste groups whose interrelationship has been exacerbated by exposure to an increasing number of forces in the modern world, among them the resurgence of religious self-consciousness and loyalty.

The thrust of this Introduction is to underscore four principal aspects of the problem of identity, each constituting a significant part of the interplay between religious and social change in South Asia. The *first* concerns numerous new features on the social, economic and political landscape (e.g., those of status, leadership, law, and rising expectations) which comprise the impact of modernity upon ancient social and ideological structures. To cite these is not to imply that significant change was absent within earlier forms of society but simply that the extent, pace and nature of change today are of a different order. The *second* aspect is that of identity itself and involves a recognition of the politically important fact that peoples the world over, in all societies, are undergoing self-examination with regard to their roots, their heritage, their ethnic, racial and religious make-up. The very ambivalence of this experience lies in the prospect of continuing cultural diversity existing along with the potential threat of renewed ethnocentrism. This fact makes the present moment of time especially confusing and volatile, yet it also provides the possibility for forms of pluralism in which different traditions respect each other. The *third* ingredient of this picture entails the examining of what strategies groups and communities use to advance their position, capture or influence power, and secure gains that are never permanently won. It is in this realm that one becomes particularly aware of social conflict, as power is sought and resisted, but the existence of conflict may be identified long before it is politically articulated and strategies are conceived. The *fourth* element consists of identifying continuing conflicts or dilemmas which result from legal changes and power shifts, leading sometimes to intensification of inter-communal rivalries and antagonism, and sometimes to the further deterioration of circumstances which are already bleak. And, within all these aspects it is important to see religious phenomena as inherently complex and ambiguous, rather than in reductionist or static terms, in order to gain insight into the role religious traditions play with respect to social conflict and to the ways in which people perceive themselves.

I

Turning to the first of these four, the new features of the socio-political landscape constituting the impact of modernity, several are alluded to in the following essays. While only a fraction of the many influences upon the modern scene, they help to highlight the problem of identity or self-image as a central element in today's social conflicts. Of these, one stands out as symbolically supreme, namely, the increasing rejection by depressed classes of a permanently debased status. One of the more dramatic contemporary instances of this rejection may be seen in the Ambedkar-led movement. As Gokhale points out, the refusal by Ambedkar to see the caste system as acceptable any longer was in fact something new in the history of Hinduism and of India, however many cries of protest had been made before by important figures over several centuries. "He was the first among the untouchables to articulate the tragedy and hopes of his people in terms of modern thought and modernistic forms of political and social action." While it was his political efforts which gave teeth to his resolve, it was his indictment of a religious system he believed could not reform itself and his vision of a future for his people (when severed from their untouchable past) that provided him with determination to seek political means to a problem that was only partly social. If the example of Ambedkar and the Mahars is more dramatic than most, the irreversible unwillingness to be disbarred from opportunity because of inherited status is of course rapidly becoming part of the scene the world over. While the fruits of such a struggle are typically slow in coming, the symbolism of the resolve is momentous.

A second feature related directly to this is the increasing reluctance of people who have been politically disenfranchised and economically impotent to have others from higher strata in society, no matter how well-intentioned, assume leadership on their behalf. Ambedkar, for instance, rejected the efforts of Mahatma Gandhi in support of the lowest castes as being inadequate and misguided. It is no accident that his own origins as an untouchable enabled him to see more clearly the path to liberation than those who had never experienced this status. One sees a similar phenomenon in the case of the Izhavas of Kerala who felt it necessary finally to exercise political power as the primary way to undo the results of low caste status endured at the hands of Namboothiri Brahmans for more than a thousand years.

Thirdly, the influence of the West and its gradually evolved more open forms of social justice were instrumental in motivating Ambedkar and the leadership among the Izhavas to seek educational, economic, political and legal means of advancing the status of scheduled castes within Indian society. The single most important instrument of Western origin was that of constitutional law, especially as shaped by British experience and as learned by Indians at home and abroad. Though Robert Baird's essay makes it evident how difficult it has been for the courts to resolve issues of a "religious" nature, there can be no doubt about the power of the Indian Constitution in defining the rights of Indian citizens. While justice can never be approximated through law alone and while laws themselves are not always just, without law justice is not possible. The impact of this new reality has been decisive.

Finally, there is one feature of the modern scene, arising from hopes generated through legal and political action, which has become highly ambiguous, even productive of disillusionment, namely, the revolution of rising expectations. The time differential between promises of social and economic justice on the one hand and actual achievement of significant gains, which come only through altered priorities and changed social institutions, can result in cynical disbelief and further grievances. This fact goes a long way to explain motivations behind the 1971 insurgency in Sri Lanka which was engaged in by those who saw no prospect of economic security but whose appetites had been whetted by unrealistic promises from all political parties. In the case of the Izhavas, however, as well as the Mahars, one sees forms of resiliency and resourcefulness developing in the face of such disillusionment, issuing in effective political and economic action. At any rate, the problems of modern society quickly trigger a revolution of falling expectations which becomes dangerous if it results in a sense of hopelessness rather than a more realistic assessment of how doggedly men cling to old priorities, how long economic development takes, what structural changes are called for, and how unending is the pursuit of social justice.

II

Central to renewed quests for identity, which constitute so much of social and political ferment today, is the necessity of coping with traditional and newly created definitions side by side. It is this which comprises the *problem* of identity, for definitions of self, community and nation are being forged out of situations where tradition and modernity make conflicting appeals, producing a rebirth of pride in one's heritage along with the determination to benefit by opportunities unknown in the past. At the heart of identity always is what it means to be a person, a community, which is a religious more than it is a social or political or ethnic issue. In fact, it is significantly religious to the very degree that it not only takes seriously these other aspects of personhood (i.e., one's communal, national, and cultural roots) but also does not bestow ultimate status upon them. This notion of what authentically religious quests for identity entail is, of course, foreign neither to ancient nor modern concepts of man; indeed, these quests prompt society to engage in self-criticism. Their role is therefore as much an *agent provocateur* as an agent of continuity, a disturber of peace no less than a provider of assurances.

Each of the essays in this collection deals with the issue of identity in one form or another. While most of them examine situations where the search for identity is profoundly religious as well as socio-political, four essays in particular explore this kind of quest explicitly, i.e., those by Gokhale, Pullapilly, O'Connell and Selvadurai. In the case of B. G. Gokhale's treatment of the movement shaped and directed by Dr. Ambedkar, architect of the Indian Constitution, we have a picture of a man whose vision for untouchables in India was no less than a total transformation of their condition, with stress as much upon their sense of dignity as persons as upon creating opportunities for their educational and economic betterment. Toward these inseparable ends he became convinced that the system which produced untouchables had no capacity to treat them in other than abusive ways and decided therefore that his people had no future within this system. Unlike many reformers, however, his conviction of what helped men discover their dignity did not include a rejection of religious meaning and traditions. While only finally deciding upon the Buddhist tradition shortly before his death in 1956, he had wrestled with this problem since 1935, considering many possibilities before believing Buddhism to be the most appropriate. It is important to stress both Ambedkar's grasp of men's deeper needs and his insight into the ways by which religious and social identity are intertwined.

In his paper Cyriac Pullapilly traces the Izhavas of Kerala from their legendary pre-outcaste status as Buddhists, prior to the influx of Namboothiri

Brahmans from the north (beginning at least a millenium ago), to their being granted low caste status within a society thoroughly revamped along Brahmanic lines, to their growing sense of renewed identity in the late nineteenth and early twentieth centuries as a community with immense political potential. Such a story is obviously complex, but one of its more interesting ingredients is the attempt made by the Izhava leader at the turn of the century, Sri Narayana Guru, to fashion a religious identity for his people *within* the Hindu fabric which would provide them access to temples and priests and festivals by creating an entire religious superstructure paralleling that from which they were excluded. To lend this cognitive support he also created a theological system, called *advaita* (non-dualist) after Shankaracarya of the ninth century, which he "verbalized in his famous slogan: 'One caste, one religion, one God,' which is today boldly inscribed on every Izhava temple, shrine, school and office." As Pullapilly indicates, however, this only served to erect a religious ghetto, further stressing their separate identity as low caste, and led eventually to more extreme disillusionment with Hinduism, prompting large numbers by 1935 to consider the conversion to other faiths. This latter step was averted only through the granting of rights by the Travancore government which allowed Izhavas regular access to state-supported temples. This step, along with the gradual socio-political gains they were making, provided a renewed sense of communal power and dignity which achieved further impetus through the national Constitution and their significant role within the Communist Party in Kerala. As in the case of Ambedkar, the most political of men, who discovered he had to weave together political and religious elements, there were those among the Izhavas who continued to see religious identity as intrinsic to their problems as low caste members of society. While it is not possible to predict the shapes Izhava identity may take in the future, it is unlikely they will be political or ethnic alone.

The essay by Joseph O'Connell deals with the identity of an entire people whose rich heritage is fed by many streams, but whose national existence has barely begun and whose cultural and religious destiny is very unclear at the present moment. Though the large Muslim majority shares much of Bengali culture with the Hindu minority (approximately 15%), the 1972 Constitution and the present political leadership under Sheikh Mujib incline Bangladesh in overly scrupulous secular directions as a state, prompted largely by fears of communalism and its divisive potential. While not without foundations, in O'Connell's estimation, these fears have the ironic effect of giving inadequate weight to the counsel of responsible Muslim laymen, thereby both depriving society of valuable insight regarding local and national problems, and stimulating Muslim self-assertiveness toward becoming more communally oriented rather than less so. Granted the delicacy of the situation politically and religiously, the point is well made that religious loyalties cannot be expected to play no part in the future of this country. A more enlightened tack would encourage discussions among Hindu and Muslim communities about their role in helping to create a viable "national identity and national purpose," in the process managing to transform potential communalism into constructive pluralism. Despite the immensity of Bangladesh's problems (e.g., mismanagement of resources, overpopulation, underemployment, etc.), the circumstances are made more serious by the failure to deal openly with the problem of national identity, which is inseparable from the religious composition of Bangladesh society.

The canvas examined by Anthony Selvadurai is on a much more limited scale (i.e., a small Sinhalese village), but the issue is also that of self-image or identity. Here the conflict results in part from persons being identified on different levels and in part from definitions of identity coming from the outside, from the law, not simply village custom. Focussing on the connections between kinship, personhood and the rights over land, he shows how custom and village elders determine all these by whether one is a "citizen" (thereby a "whole person") or whether one is an "outsider" (a "part person" though still living in the village). These categories arise by virtue of membership traced through the male lineage to an ancestor who founded the village two centuries ago. While the village is a one-caste community, these two categories amount to a sharp hierarchical cleavage and inevitably effect not only each person's social rights but his very sense of identity. In disputes over land an "outsider" sometimes resorts to legal action, though not frequently because of its high cost in time and money, in order to define inheritance rights and land use not by village practice but on impartial terms before the law. The threat litigation constitutes to the community is one amounting to challenging the basis of order itself and in the process sorcery is often resorted to as a way of arresting this fundamental invasion and of counteracting the force of outside law. The deep nature of the conflict is further revealed by the fact that even vindication of equal property rights before the law cannot grant citizenship status to one considered as a "part person" within the community. This is another reminder that law alone is insufficient to alter social structures and behavior, but it is also testimony to the considerable power law can have in shaking the foundations of what had previously been regarded as unassailable. While religious traditions can be made to defend the status quo *or* to assail it, the cleavage between "whole" and "part" people ultimately becomes indefensible when exposed to different bases on which the identity of persons is established. That religion frequently supports this sort of cleavage attests to its social origins, but that it has also attacked such violations of human dignity attests to its potential independence of customary norms.

Two other examples of the struggle for identity and the attempt on the part of persons either to reinforce or to reconceive their role in society may be seen in the essays by H. L. Seneviratne and Agehananda Bharati, both of which deal with the present scene within Sri Lanka. In the one instance, there is the continuing tension between Kandyan aristocrats and low-country bureaucrats, originating in the British colonial period which favored the latter over the former; in the other, there is the growing dilemma within Ceylonese society of a political, educational and social elite which remains unable to motivate and train its young to serve the real needs of the nation because it persists in making promises it cannot keep and refuses to pursue realistic and essential priorities. While the analysis by Bharati and others of the social origins and economic status both of young people engaged in the insurgency and of monks who supported this cause makes it clear that economic considerations were paramount, one may also argue that a nation's failure to create mechanisms for involving its young in addressing chronic social needs is a religious as well as a political problem, revealing a society's unwillingness to make fundamental changes. This is not a question of tradition versus modernity, any more than it is an issue limited to Ceylon, to South Asia, or to developing societies.

III

Among the most interesting and politically significant modern phenomena is the relationship between a community's self-image and the strategies it employs for effective social change. One approach to understanding this relationship is to suggest a spectrum along which to view all seven essays in this collection as well as the topic more broadly. This spectrum would run the gamut from violent attempts to seize power on the left to assorted policies on the right designed to abort substantial shifts in power. In between may be found positions representing a variety of tensions, i.e., between those which are conflict-oriented and those stressing consensus, between those provoking accelerated change and those content with evolutionary progress, and between the more ideologically bound and those tending toward pragmatism. It is obvious that any such spectrum contains overlapping positions and the combining of stances and strategies, varying with the circumstances, the experience of those in leadership, and the effectiveness of methods already used. I am assuming also that part of what is at stake here is the quest for a new identity, not simply access to power and its advantages. The role of religious loyalties and symbols among these tensions is therefore potentially pertinent and may be used to justify either radical or ultra-conservative measures and policies. Again, religious traditions lend themselves to a variety of ends (e.g., rise in status, political unification, legitimation of power), though man's religious quests may also raise serious questions about values, goals and procedures which have implications for political policy and action. In any case, religious affiliations must be seen as essential components in understanding the arenas of social conflict.

It is commonplace in political struggles for violence and extremism to be found at both ends of any such spectrum, stemming to a large degree from disillusionment, despair and the conviction that other means of resolving situations do not exist. From the standpoint of conservatives, extremists are always on the left; to radicals, violent action is appropriate response to other forms of violence inflicted on those without power. It is also a commonplace that radicals of one generation become the conservatives of the next, though it is not uncommon for normally apolitical men to become radicalized by situations of despair. A perfect example of the latter exists in the 1971 insurgency in Sri Lanka where very non-radical young people from economically unpromising backgrounds became convinced that none of the existing political parties (including those putatively Marxist in orientation) was interested in challenging in any fundamental way what is essentially an inbred social system furthering the advantages of the elite at the expense of much needed social and economic change.[1] Not only was the Bandaranaike government in power, despite its leftist rhetoric, shocked by the actions of the insurgents who were presumed to be supporters of the government, but there was further alarm over the amount of popular sympathy which backed the cause of these young people, if not their radical tactics. However quelled the insurgents, the despair and anger which accompanied their radicalization is handwriting on the wall about the mounting disenchantment with a political elite whose policies are not geared to make substantive change. In this sense, it bears similarity to the despair experienced by Ambedkar and other untouchables in India who became convinced that a form of radicalism, i.e., separation of themselves from the system which excluded them from full identity, was the only sane alternative.

At the other end of political spectrums exist governments, communally-oriented organizations, and other social groups which see disorder and the threat of chaos as the primary danger and strong control of these forces as their mandate. The temptation of those in power to justify severe forms of repression and to lack sensitivity to the plight of the powerless hardly needs documentation in our era. The phenomenon is of one piece with the Ceylonese scene just cited, with the experience of the Mahars and Izhavas within the Indian caste structure, and with the current crushing of "opponents, real or imagined, with sledgehammer tactics" that is reported from Bangladesh. The counsels of despair that issue in retaliatory reaction to political threat are no less part of the problems involving identity than those forms of despair coming from below. Both types are caught in an atmosphere of panic, seeing basic change from opposite camps. In part, the fundamental religious question is not how to avoid or permanently resolve social conflict but what resources need to be employed in such situations that will help all segments of society discover increased self-respect through more widespread balancing of power and by the sharing of responsibility.

In between these extremes lies the lifeblood of political affairs, the carving of strategies and mechanisms to maintain basic order at the same time that society responds remedially to those in need. Here the alternatives are not kill or be killed, but whether particular policies and stratagems are effective in

---

1   See Gananath Obeyesekere, "Some Comments on the Social Backgrounds of the April 1971 Insurgency in Sri Lanka (Ceylon)," *Journal of Asian Studies*, Vol. XXXIII, No. 3 (May 1974), pp. 367–384. In this he analyzes a very large data base collected on those engaged in or actively sympathetic with the insurgency. Also, he examines the context out of which this movement emerged and makes a strong case for the "alienation of the elite from the rest of the country".

coping with complex and frequently intractable issues in a context where there are always contending parties. Each of the following essays deals implicitly or directly with this reality. In the center of political activity may be seen the efforts of individuals and groups to further their own welfare by constitutional, legislative, economic and educational means. The resort to litigation, the capturing and exercizing of political power, the lobbying and striking for economic improvement, and the pursuit of training and expertise through education are all conventional and familiar channels by which communities become upwardly mobile and power is distributed. While less dramatic than more extreme tactics, these reveal the normality of social conflict in equally clear outline and provide even more effective paths toward the achievement of durable status.

If the mainstream of political activity encourages the envisioning of power as something to be shared among men, however unequally, it also presumes that the sharing of authority results in the potential enhancement of human dignity. Once more, the issue has religious dimensions at its core. As Ambedkar made it clear, his concern was for the total transformation of untouchable status, from being despised castes in a society which saw them as religiously inferior, i.e., outside the caste system (*avarna*), to a newly discovered status of full equality in human terms. The same impetus lay behind the efforts of the Izhavas in Kerala who were concerned not simply with improved political and economic conditions but with full access to all forms of human dignity. Again, the various forms of constitutional rights and litigation discussed below in the contexts of India, Bangladesh and Sri Lanka have as their basic assumption that equality before the law stems from a more basic status which transcends social and political definitions of identity. While there is nothing nefarious about the balancing and exercizing of power, the process becomes self-defeating and inhumane when it fails to recognize that its goal is human welfare, not increased power per se. History reminds one how frequently social conflict results from unresolved problems of communal identity and how these problems at their deepest level involve the meaning of personhood and corporate existence.

IV

If those possessing power are frequently insensitive to the plight of the powerless, it is sometimes the illusion of those seeking power that gains in legal rights, political consciousness and educational opportunities will remedy social injustice. In reality, since power is always relative, alert political awareness often makes visible new dilemmas which may be more subtle, more intense and doubly frustrating. This final section is an effort on my part to pose some of these dilemmas on a general level and to relate them to what has been said before. While these dilemmas are essentially worldwide in scope, their consequences are especially serious for South Asian countries at the present time.

In an era when the "rich get richer" it is small consolation for the poor to make gains which are not commensurate with the problems of deteriorating economic conditions (of increasing poverty with its substandard housing, inadequate diet and underemployment) and with the prospect of more serious economic and social dislocations ahead. The gains which have come to the dispossessed within the past few decades (however important in legal, political and economic terms) are in no way adequate to meet the dilemmas of the next generation. While the problems of South Asia are not unique, there is a magnitude about them which gives grounds for despair. Those who are optimistic about the immediate or long-term future in India, Bangladesh or Sri Lanka rarely speak to convinced audiences. While apocalyptic visions are often Western in origin, they are commonly drawn from the discouraged pictures presented by realistic members of those countries. In brief form what are the dilemmas which cannot be wished away during the next several decades but must be faced honestly and worked at with all the resources that are available? Needless to say, these questions are posed not out of gratuitousness but out of recognition that they have implications far beyond South Asia.

1. In situations where educational opportunities enable large numbers of young people to complete not only secondary school but university level and yet where economic stagnancy creates inadequate employment possibilities, how does a society deal with the problems of understandable anger, frustration, and of wasted human resources? This dilemma is of crisis proportions in Ceylon, but it has its special forms everywhere, including economically developed countries. The clash between rising expectations and falling opportunities breeds cynicism especially when the young see that connections and not ability determine one's chances for positions and advancement. (Obeyesekere's article on the 1971 insurgency is important on this score.) Under these circumstances the conflict between furthering one's own interests and being concerned for the needs of society becomes more marked, arising from the observation that society rewards not the meritorious but those who learn the ways of manipulation.

2. While no nation or community can develop its human and natural resources, its institutional and cultural assets, without relying upon elites of various sorts, how does a society prevent its elites from becoming self-perpetuating in the worst sense? The dilemma of combining circulation of the elite with the necessity for encouraging trained, competent and responsible elites is, of course, crucial to all modern societies. The choice is not between these but how to further security and continuity on the one hand and reasonably open access on the other. Unfortunately, elites often solve their political problems by asking others to make sacrifices and by creating convenient scapegoats which serve to reinforce their own positions. For those who are denied access to power and decision-making, especially the young with ability, patterns of leadership which are basically self-serving ultimately backfire and invite violent revolution.

3. Among the consequences of stimulating the political consciousness of previously non-politicized segments of any society is the necessity of including

enough representatives from these segments in decisionmaking echelons before political awareness turns to disillusion. As mentioned earlier, one central feature of modern times is the growing insistence by the poor not only to have their own representatives but that these persons be involved in policy decisions effecting their lives. This is obviously what democratic government is all about, but the present dilemma throughout the world is how to accomplish this with dispatch now that political consciousness has been activated in unprecedented ways.

4. In present economic circumstances, which do not permit the luxury of unlimited open competition and where difficult decisions about priorities need to be made, how does leadership combine sufficient control over society's principal choices without undermining the basic freedoms of its citizens, especially the right to challenge inappropriate options? How, in other words, to combine society's twofold need of exercising control over its basic functioning and of remaining receptive to fundamental critique? The helplessness with which citizens in all countries today look upon the decision-making process as it copes with problems of enormous complexity gives one the impression that there is little difference between democratic societies and those with no pretenses about having governments that are accountable. The era of technocrats and byzantine-like bureaucracy creates a major dilemma which strikes at the heart of modern society. In a real sense, it is as problematic to elites as to those groups without political or economic influence.

5. Arising from recent as well as ancient experience of racial, religious and ethnic forms of communalism there has emerged the dilemma of how to fashion forms of local, national and international cohesiveness (enabling communities to transcend more narrow definitions of identity) without creating forms of identification which do violence to how they construe themselves as persons. The more serious the political and economic problems, the greater is the temptation to fashion a basis of cooperation which does injustice to the diversity of ethnic and religious traditions. There is considerable evidence, however, that forms of cohesiveness which disregard these traditions are short-lived. In fact, the ignoring of resources within social, cultural and religious traditions invites an impoverishment of perspectives as well as stimulates the communal antagonisms they seek to avoid.

6. Lastly, on the global scene, where major problems show little respect for national borders or political ideology, lies the dilemma of how to cope with the inequities between *rich* and *poor* nations without resort to conventional forms of violence or increased patterns of blackmail. In the minds of politically active persons from third world countries the principal problem today is not overpopulation or pollution control or agricultural yield, however critical these may be, but social justice, i.e., the more equitable distribution of financial and natural resources and the creation of political and economic structures which ensure the eventual closing of gaps between the haves and the have-nots. While some see this as a simple transference of control, the most vivid example of the dilemma lies in the debate between those advocating population control

(usually from the West) and those arguing for economic development (normally from underdeveloped countries) as the answer to problems of impending world famine. The point here is that persons on both sides of this debate seek to resolve the dilemma by ignoring various of its components, despite the fact that "more than a decade of experience is available to document the proposition that programs directed to economic development and to population growth *are* mutually supportive."[2]

In conclusion, the above examples of dilemmas facing mankind not only entail intense social conflict but ultimately involve broader questions of communal and national identity. While religious traditions may or may not address themselves to these sorts of issues, the problem at its deepest is inescapably religious, for the identity of persons is corporate as well as individual in nature. And, if so, the dignity of no one is finally enhanced except by working for the dignity of all. This is as true of communities, even of national communities in the present time, as of individuals. The basically interdependent nature of the modern world makes a cooperative approach to these dilemmas fundamental to their resolution.

---

2 See the article by Michael S. Teitelbaum, "Population and Development: Is a Consensus Possible?", *Foreign Affairs*, July, 1974, pp. 742–760. In this carefully reasoned piece he makes the case that "there is no empirical warrant for the 'either/or' type of argument" but that there is a growing international consensus which "holds that policies and programs are required *both* for general development *and* for specific population concerns, and that these complementary efforts ought to be components of all international development assistance."

Dr. Bhimrao Ramji Ambedkar: Rebel against Hindu Tradition

BALKRISHNA GOVIND GOKHALE

Wake Forest University, Winston Salem, North Carolina, U.S.A.

FOR ALMOST three decades (1928–1956) Bhimrao Ramji Ambedkar (1891–1956) was an unrelenting challenge to Hindu dogma and social practices. To most political leaders, including M. K. Gandhi (1869–1948) and Jawaharlal Nehru (1889–1964), he was a troublesome spectre casting a menacing shadow over their grand national designs. To the orthodox Hindu he was anathema, an "untouchable" who persistently refused "to keep his place." To millions of his followers he was a "father figure," *Babasaheb* as he was fondly and reverently addressed, a veritable saviour vindicating their human rights and heroically striving to lift them out of the mire of poverty and degradation into which the Hindu social system had cast them. Cram-full of facts, vitriolic in his denunciations, unbending in his personal and general likes and dislikes, tireless in his energy and prophetic in his pronouncements, Ambedkar symbolised a unique phenomenon in the political and social history of modern India.

It is too early to deliver definitive judgment on the longevity and vitality of Ambedkar's impact upon Hinduism. In its characteristic way Hinduism epitomised him as its "modern Manu" and promptly laid his ghost to rest. Ambedkar had challenged Hinduism where it was most vulnerable, the caste system and its correlate – untouchability. The bastions of the system have begun to show cracks, but it will be a long time before they will crumble if recent studies are any indication.[1] As his final riposte, Ambedkar led millions of his followers into a new religion (Buddhism) in October 1956 in the hope that they would escape the tyranny of the caste system thereby. But in hundreds of villages in Maharashtra they simply seem to have exchanged one label for another, for now they are taken to be "untouchable" Buddhists![2]

---

1 For such studies see Irawati Karve, *Hindu Society-An Interpretation* (Poona, 1961), pp. 159–161; Devabrata Bose, *The Problems of Indian Society* (Bombay, 1968), pp. 184 ff.; André Betéille, *Castes: Old and New* (Bombay, 1969), pp. 95–102; James Silverberg (Ed.), *Social Mobility In The Caste System In India* (The Hague, 1968), pp. 135–136; Lloyd I. Rudolph and Susanne H. Rudolph, *The Modernity of Tradition* (Chicago, 1967), pp. 129 ff.
2 See Eleanor Zelliot, "The Revival of Buddhism in India" in *Asia*: A Journal Published by the Asia Society (New York, 1968), No. 10; Winter, 1968, pp. 33–45, especially p. 45.

The phenomenon called Ambedkar, however, cannot be dismissed as inconsequential, a starry flash of lightning illumining the darkness covering the lower orders of Hindu society. His life and leadership symbolise something new in the history of Hinduism and India. The dimensions of his challenge to Hinduism were altogether of a new order. There have been cries of protest in behalf of the millions of the suppressed sections of Hindu society in the past; witness the impressive list of "saint-poets" of Maharashtra for such protests. These were Namadeva (1270–1350), a tailor; Narahari, a goldsmith; Sawanta, the gardener; Gora, the potter; and most of all Chokha, the Mahar (the caste to which Ambedkar belonged). These occupy a place of pride in the Bhakti tradition,[3] though the bases of their protests were entirely different. They took their stand on the metaphysical and theological assumption of the Bhakti tradition securely moored in the *Vedanta* and called upon God to redress wrongs done to their fellow humans by the priests and other entrenched religious and social interests. They meekly stood outside the temple doors and patiently waited for someone to pour water into their joined palms to quench their thirst on a searing day. Ambedkar was no meek supplicant; he led his followers to the shores of a forbidden lake to draw water for themselves and attempted to push himself through the temple doors into the forbidden sanctum. He demanded his rights in terms of the natural rights of man, in terms of social justice and ethical integrity. He was the first among the untouchables to articulate the tragedy and hopes of his people in terms of modern thought and modernistic forms of political and social action. He exposed the tyrannies perpetrated not only by the Brahmans but also the non-Brahman upper castes such as the Marathas (the dominant caste in rural Maharashtra) and, adroitly using his political strength rooted in the unflinching devotion of his followers, put the untouchables on the political map of India and on the collective conscience of Hindu leadership, liberal and orthodox. In a sense, therefore, Ambedkar's rebellion against Hinduism was the symbol of the impact of modernity on Hindu tradition.

II

Ambedkar's career may be briefly summarized at the outset. He was born in the Mahar caste, a rather numerous (about three million in numbers) untouchable caste in Maharashtra, parts of Madhya Pradesh and Andhra Pradesh. He was born in the family of the Sakpals (the name Ambedkar was acquired either from the native family village of Ambavade or "gifted" to him by a Brahman teacher) two generations of whom had taken to military service under the British. Enrollment in the British-Indian army was used as a means of upward economic and social mobility by many Mahars during the second half of the nineteenth and first four decades of the twentieth

---

3 For details see H. S. Shenolikar, *Pracheen Marathi Vangmayanche Swaroop* (Kolhapur, 1962), pp. 72 ff.; D. K. Kelkar, *Marathi Sahityanche Simhavalokana* (Poona, 1963), pp. 95 ff.

century. Ambedkar was born in Mhow in Madhya Pradesh on April 14, 1891, the fourteenth child of Ramji Sakpal and his wife Bhimabai (née Murbadkar, a daughter of a Mahar noncommissioned officer of the Indian army). He received his early education in Dapoli and Satara and graduated from the Elphinstone High School in Bombay in 1907. Before his high school graduation Ambedkar was married to Ramabai, daughter of Mr. Bhiku Walangkar who worked as a porter at Dapoli.[4] With the help of a scholarship given him by the Maharaja of Baroda, Ambedkar went to the Elphinstone College in Bombay and received his B.A. degree from the University of Bombay in 1912. Once again with the assistance of a scholarship from the native state of Baroda, Ambedkar went to Columbia University in New York in 1913, receiving his M.A. in 1915. In 1916 he went to London to become a Barrister-at-Law but had to return to India in August 1917 as the scholarship could not be extended. After a brief spell of work for the Baroda State administration, Ambedkar went to live in Bombay where he taught in a business school of the Sydenham College of Commerce and the Government Law College to augment his meagre earnings from his law practice. He returned to London in 1920, this time with a scholarship from the Maharaja of Kolhapur, another native state. In London he completed his work for Barrister-at-Law and a D.Sc. in Economics and returned to India in 1923.

From the ghettos of Bombay Ambedkar had travelled far. His academic achievements were brilliant on any count but more so in the context of his social origins. He was the first untouchable to graduate from high school, the first to receive a B.A. from an Indian university, the first to get graduate degrees from Columbia and London, and the first to be Barrister-at-Law. These distinctions were beyond the wildest dreams of an untouchable youth. His college and foreign education was made possible by generous financial assistance from the two Maharajas of Baroda and Kolhapur, but Ambedkar used his exceptional opportunities well and assiduously. He practised law in Bombay but increasingly became involved in the social and political movements that were then mobilising the non-Brahmans and untouchable castes. Between 1924 and 1940 Ambedkar played the role of a stormy petrel in Indian politics. He constantly feuded with the Indian National Congress, and especially Mahatma Gandhi, challenging their right to speak in the name of the untouchables and questioning their sincerity in doing anything far-reaching for the betterment of the social and economic position of the millions of untouchables. He felt that Gandhi was just sweeping the problem of the untouchables under the capacious rug of the Hindu caste system with his own interpretation of the *Varna* system and calling the untouchables *Harijans*, or "People of God." Ambedkar felt that the problem was much too deep-rooted and complex to be solved through simplistic social reform, for it needed a total

---

4 Biographical details are based on Dhananjay Keer, *Dr. Ambedkar-Life and Mission* (Bombay, 1962); see page 14 for the name Ambedkar. For details of the origins and development of the Mahar movement see Eleanor Mae Zelliot, *Dr. Ambedkar and the Mahar Movement* (unpublished Ph.D. dissertation, University of Pennsylvania, 1969).

change in Hindu thinking and a comprehensive transformation in the Hindu social structure. Caste, to Ambedkar, was not something that Hinduism acquired in an adventitious manner but represented the very core of Hinduism and wherever caste functioned, as a part and parcel of a theologically sanctioned institution, there had to be "outcastes."

Through his movements Ambedkar thought he could make his followers politically conscious and unite for concerted action in securing their basic human rights. In 1935 he shocked the Hindus by announcing his intention to seek conversion to Christianity, Islam, or Sikhism as a means of escape for his people from the tyranny of Hinduism. During World War II he served as a Member of the Governor-General's Executive Council and after the advent of independence became Law Minister in the Nehru cabinet. He was responsible for drafting the constitution of the Republic of India, for which he was hailed as the "Modern Manu." His defeat in the elections of 1952 practically marked the end of his political career; deteriorating health and increasing frustration finally led him on October 14, 1956 to convert himself to Buddhism along with millions of his followers. He did not live long thereafter, for he died on December 6, 1956 in New Delhi. His funeral in Bombay was attended by half a million sorrowing people.

III

Mention has been made of the unique character of Ambedkar's rebellion earlier. It is difficult to separate the immediate and political aspects of his rebellion from those which should be regarded as more fundamental in their historical implication. For almost thirty years Ambedkar played a dramatic role in Indian politics and his politics overshadowed the ideological and cultural aspects of his rebellion. His conversion to Buddhism symbolised the ultimate state in this rebellion.

Ambedkar's rebellion must be understood both in the context of the circumstances of his life and his personal intellectual and spiritual development. In many ways he was so untypical of the average untouchable. Even as a Mahar he was untypical. Ambedkar's family, as mentioned earlier, had taken to military service and risen far beyond the average Mahar in an average Maharashtra village. Military service meant opportunities of living outside the confines of Hindu society, of educational opportunities for children of Mahar army men, of contact with the British, and experience of wide travel in India. Ambedkar's sojourn in the West added another and powerful dimension to his life and thought. It lifted him far above not only his own caste but numerous others from the higher castes in terms of higher education and cultural sophistication. Most of his life was spent in large urban centers such as Bombay, New York, and London. By dint of his education and efforts he had become the most influential spokesman for his people and his views were listened to with concern, if not respect, both by the British Government and leaders of the Indian National Congress. This was particularly true of nationalist leaders such as Gandhi and Nehru. During his years of leadership he lived in Dadar, a middleclass upper caste Hindu residential suburban area of Bombay, and for most of the time, whether professionally or politically, he dealt with the upper strata of Hindu and Indian society.

The three dominant influences in Ambedkar's life were the religious spirit of his family which influenced his early childhood, the humiliations he suffered at the hands of higher caste Hindus as a student and a professional person in India, and the six-plus years he spent in the West (in the U.S. and England). Each of these shaped his thinking and determined his reactions to religion and political events in India.

In religious affiliations Ambedkar's family belonged to the *Kabir Panth*. The Saint Kabir lived during the last quarter of the fifteenth and the opening decades of the sixteenth century. (Tradition asserts that he died in A.D. 1518.) He was a disciple of Ramananda who infused a new life into the Bhakti movement initiated by the great Ramanuja. Kabir attacked caste distinctions as also religious differences and preached the gospel of loving devotion to the One and Loving God.[5] During his early childhood, Ambedkar must have listened to the devotional songs sung very early in the morning by the older women folk in the household. The spirit of Bhakti as reflected in the Kabir tradition had a lasting influence on Ambedkar's life, for just before his death in New Delhi on December 6, 1956 he is reported to have hummed a song of Kabir.[6] It is worth remembering that this was some months after his formal conversion to Buddhism. How this element of Bhakti in Ambedkar was related to other aspects of his thinking will be discussed later.

The Kabir Panthis and the untouchables in general live on the periphery of the diverse traditions of Hinduism. If the Vedic tradition be called the Classical Tradition, then the religion of the village folk, as made manifest in the worship of local deities, may be described as the "Little Tradition." In between stands another which, for want of a better or more precise nomenclature, may be termed the "Middle Tradition." This "Middle" tradition is based on the translations and versions of the Sanskrit Puranas and the epics (*Ramayana* and *Mahabharata*) in the regional languages (Marathi, Gujarati, Bengali, Hindi and a host of others) where they undergo subtle but significant changes as they become related to regional traditions in thinking and customs. The "Saint-poets" of Maharashtra, such as Namadeva and Chokha Mela, belonged to this "Middle" tradition as they expressed their religious feelings and thoughts in terms of the theistic-pantheistic-mystical concepts so characteristic of the Bhakti tradition in Hindu India.[7] Caste prejudices and tyranny

5 For Kabir and his teachings see R. C. Majumdar (Ed.), *The Delhi Sultanate* 1960), pp. 560–566; G. H. Westcott, *Kabir and the Panth* (Calcutta, 1953); Rabindranath Tagore, *Songs of Kabir* (New York, 1916); for the influence of the Bhakti tradition among the Mahars see Alexander Robertson, *The Mahar Folk* (Calcutta, 1938), Chapter VII.
6 Keer, *op. cit.*, p. 510.
7 For the ideological contents of this tradition in Maharashtra see S. V. Dandekar in *Maharashtreeya Santa - Vangmaya va Jeevana* (Bombay, 1952), pp. 21–28; D. K. Kelkar, *op. cit.*, pp. 101–111; for Chokha Mela, see Robertson, *op. cit.*, pp. 80–91.

prevented Ambedkar from learning Sanskrit during his high school career; consequently, he had very few opportunities to establish emotional or intellectual relationships with the ideological contents of any of the three traditions of Hinduism in an effective manner. What he retained was a somewhat mystical/devotional attitude which expressed itself in his speeches and exhortations to his people and in his intensely personal thoughts.

The humiliations inflicted on him by the caste Hindus created in Ambedkar a substratum of intense bitterness and hostility toward the Hindu tradition as a whole. Writing in 1948, Ambedkar expressed his views on the character of Hinduism as a civilization in the most categorical way. He referred to the existence of the so-called Criminal Tribes, the Aboriginal Tribes, and the Untouchables and their treatment by the caste Hindus. He said: "The Hindu Civilization, gauged in the light of these social products, could hardly be called civilization. It is a diabolical contrivance to suppress and enslave humanity. Its proper name would be Infamy. What else can be said of a civilization which has produced a mass of people who are taught to accept crime as an approved means of earning their livelihood, another mass of people who are left to live in full bloom of their primitive barbarism in the midst of civilization and a third mass of people who are treated as an entity beyond human intercourse and whose mere touch is enough to cause pollution?"[8] This is far different from the imploring protests of Chokha Mela as he stood outside the temple gates and wondered why the great and loving God should inflict upon him and his kin such humiliation. For Ambedkar, Hinduism was beyond reform and in his constant arguments with Gandhi he pointedly referred to the iniquitous social premises of Hinduism which could not be changed simply by giving the untouchables a new name such as Harijans (Children of God) as Gandhi did. In ages past Hinduism had failed in producing a Voltaire for the class that could produce a Voltaire, the Brahmans, had a stake in the maintenance of the caste system with themselves at its apex.[9] He had lost faith in Hinduism's ability to reform itself to the extent of eliminating the caste system with which untouchability was inevitably linked. Theological or metaphysical arguments were worse than useless even if Ambedkar could indulge in them successfully and was inclined to do so by his intellectual inclinations. These latter were a product of the modern West and these significantly influenced the character of his rebellion and its forms.

It was only in New York and London that Ambedkar could feel completely secure against social discrimination on the grounds of his caste as an untouchable. There he had experienced and enjoyed the thrust and parry of rational thought and discussion, of ideas of social revolt and change, of equality between man and man. It was also in the West that he had seen the power and capabilities of democratic politics through which underprivileged classes could secure their own rightful share of social, economic, and political power. On

---

8   B. R. Ambedkar, *The Untouchables* (Gonda, 1969), p. ix.
9   *Ibid.*, p. xi.

his return to India he had noticed the beginning of such democratic movements which, in spite of Gandhi's infusion of spiritual concepts and values, were plainly aimed at capturing power. The Indo-British system contained within itself frustrations as well as promises and Ambedkar was convinced that these promises could not be secured for his people only through movements which may be labelled reformist. Among these were the movements for using the forbidden waters of public wells and lakes, of entering temples and even consigning to a bonfire the *Book of Manu* in 1927. In 1935 he declared that he would call upon the untouchables to leave the Hindu fold and seek conversion to some other religion as the only means of escaping tyranny of the Hindu caste system. During all these years he was busy organizing the untouchables as a distinct political group with their own and separate aspirations and demands. He had discovered that his movements of reform, aimed at elimination of discrimination against the untouchables in the matter of the use of public wells and tanks and temple-entry, had only symbolic results. For the average untouchable little had changed in the villages except that now they were called Harijans. Ambedkar felt that the ruling classes in Hindu society were not so much interested in a rational reconstructing of their society as in capturing political power. His writings on the historical origins and development of the institution of untouchability tended to be dismissed as polemical outbursts of an obdurate and unreasonable leader of a minority community.[10]

Gandhi's mysticism and attempt to solve stubborn social problems through spiritual means provoked the rationalist in Ambedkar either to lofty disdain or angry denunciation. Increasingly, he had despaired of initiating any significant reform movement within Hinduism. He was also convinced that such a reform movement, in order to be effective, must reach the villages, a task which would take decades, if not centuries. He also despised village life[11] as a sink of inequity and tyranny for the lower orders of society and advised his followers to leave the rural areas in favour of urban centers. Traditional Hinduism is entrenched in its strongest form in the villages. Ambedkar stated that "To the Untouchable, Hinduism is a veritable chamber of horrors. The sanctity and infallibility of the Vedas, Smritis, Shastras, the iron law of caste, the heartless law of karma and the senseless law of status by birth are to the Untouchables veritable instruments of torture which Hinduism has forged against the Untouchables."[12]

Ambedkar also differed profoundly from Gandhi on the subject of "modernization." Gandhi denounced the machine and characterised the modern industrial civilization created by it as "Satanic." Ambedkar found Gandhi's economic ideas simplistic. He admitted that modern society did suffer from

10 For Ambedkar's opinion on Gandhi's efforts in behalf of the untouchables see his *What Congress and Gandhi Have Done To The Untouchables* (Bombay, 1946).
11 For Ambedkar's views on the village and comments on them see David G. Mandelbaum, *Society In India* (Berkeley, 1970), II, p. 356.
12 *What Congress* etc...., pp. 307–308.

imbalances wherein the rich became richer and the poor poorer, but that was the fault of systems of social organization rather than the machine itself. He seems to have developed an unbounded faith in "modernization" through which alone, he felt, the untouchables could possibly find deliverance. Modernization meant industrialization, urbanization and education, and he exhorted his followers to take to education, reform their age-old habits of thought and forms of life-style, leave the villages, go into the great cities and work out their own solutions to the problems of social inequality, discrimination and tyranny imposed on them by Hindu society.[13] He was convinced that the untouchables were not going to make any headway by begging for concessions, but if they organized themselves politically they could become a force to reckon with. He wanted them to adopt modern methods of social and political organization and draw upon the strength of their numbers (by no means negligible) and through the Western democratic process secure their own rightful place in Indian affairs. He was aware that this was a long, arduous, and painful process especially in the face of caste Hindu opposition and the untouchables' own ingrained habits of thought and attitudes. But the task had to be accomplished. He stressed education as the one powerful means of uplift for the untouchables and he went on organizing institutions of higher learning for their benefit. By the time he had ended his earthly mission he could show creditable achievements with respect to the ratio of urbanization for the untouchables (21% of their total population); also, the number of industrial workers among the Mahars were 138, 519 as against 117, 714 classified as farmers and farm-labor in Maharashtra.[14] Education too showed distinct gains, especially when viewed in the context of gains made by non-Mahars among the untouchables and even among the non-untouchable "low" castes. The status of the Mahars had visibly improved between 1927, when Ambedkar began his movement, and 1956 when he passed away. He had secured for them valuable political concessions such as "reserved" seats in the legislatures and government jobs in addition to valuable concessions in land distribution, rural credit, and investments in agriculture and business.

IV

Attacks on Hindu social traditions and acceptance of modernization were the two dominant means adopted by Ambedkar in his crusade in behalf of the untouchables. These meant a de-emphasis on religion. It would have been quite in character with his movement if it had finally resulted in a certain loss of "religiosity" among his followers. That Ambedkar was aware of this possibility is evident from his speeches and writings. For a rationalist such a loss could not be alarming and far from a fatal circumstance. But Ambedkar had within him a deep sense of the spiritual and his vision of the future of his own

13   For his views on modernization see *Ibid.*, pp. 293 ff.; for his ideas on reform of untouchable society see Keer, *op. cit.*, pp. 70, 81 *passim.*
14   See *Census Of India* (Delhi, 1961), 1961, I, Pt. II-C (i), p. 482; Pt. V-A(i), pp. 36, 37.

people was not just in terms of economic advance, social equality, or political bargains. This spiritual element in his consciousness was often deeply overlaid with bitterness and anger for, as he said, "Untouchability bids fair to last as long as Hinduism will last."[15] In October 1935 he announced publicly that he was contemplating turning his back on Hinduism and seeking for himself and his followers the solace of another faith. He considered Christianity, Islam, and Sikhism as alternatives, and 15 years later, in 1950, he had begun to think of Buddhism seriously. What had led him to seek another religion when he had such bitter feelings about Hinduism, the faith he was born in and which had, however, slowly begun to take cognisance of the problem of the untouchables and had begun to take the first and perhaps hesitant steps to redress the wrong? In an answer to this lies an aspect of Ambedkar's rebellion.

What Ambedkar was seeking for his people was more than the mere removal of the stigma attached to untouchability and the economic and social degradation inflicted by the institution upon his people. He wanted a total transformation in their lives, a new identity, a new culture. He was aware that by their conversion to other faiths or their espousal of Marxism they would create more and serious problems for themselves either as new minorities or turn themselves to a new tyranny under a "Dictatorship" that would use them and exploit them as ruthlessly, if not worse, than Hinduism had done. Secondly, he knew that the untouchables were a deeply religious people whose spiritual hunger had to be satisfied only by offering them an alternate system of religious precepts, values and ritual if they were not to be transformed into a rootless mass. He was aware that the untouchables themselves were divided into numerous castes whose regimen was as rigorous, in matters of marriage at least, as the other castes among the Hindus. He wanted them to be rid of the incubus of caste in their body-social and he felt that this could be done only through Buddhism.

Buddhism, as he understood it, was a rational creed whose founder had fought the Brahmans and the caste system; that Buddhism had created a great and glorious cultural tradition. By turning to Buddhism the untouchables could exchange their nameless and sorrowful past for a golden age of the Buddhist history which would strengthen their pride in themselves as Buddhists and create for them a sense of a new identity and new destiny. Furthermore, Buddhism was within the mainstream of the Indic tradition and had acquired prestige among sections of the Indian intellectuals. He was a rationalist enough to understand that all that passed muster as Buddhism was not without blemishes and he was particularly disturbed by the more or less total otherworldliness of the *Samgha*, with the monks and nuns working for their own salvation without much concern for the problems and ills of the world. He began to offer his own interpretation of Buddhism, an interpretation which

---

15 B. R. Ambedkar, *Mr. Gandhi And The Emancipation Of The Untouchables* (Bombay 1943), p. 12.

would purge it of what he called excrescences but retain the high ethical and spiritual values.[16] Hopefully, conversion to Buddhism would take the untouchables out of the caste system, and create for them an honorable place in the cultural life of India. Given the pace of their urbanization, industrialization and education, Buddhism would, in the course of time, create for them a new world of hope, dignity, and spiritual riches that would not be possible for them as Hindus whatever the rate of progress offered them by the social and political movements of his time. It was his own spiritual hunger and his awareness of the spiritual needs of his followers that finally led him into Buddhism. The rebel within marched out of the fold but assured the Hindus that he was close enough to them as their equal in the contributions of his new faith to the making of Indian culture. Once again we return to the image of the Mahar "saint-poet" Chokha Mela. The new Chokha Mela ceased imploring God to soften the hearts of the Brahmans so that he could get a glimpse of the idol; he had turned away from the temple itself and found his way into a new, but not too distant, shrine. Buddhism became another means of "modernization" as an instrument for the cultural transformation of the lowliest of the low in India.

That his call for conversion to Buddhism was heeded in great numbers is evident from the census figures. In 1951 there were 2,487 Buddhists in Maharashtra forming 0.1% of the total population. In 1961 the figure jumped to 2,789,501 and 7.5% of the total population far exceeding the numbers of Christians (1961 – 560,594 or 1.42% of total population) and almost coming close to the figures for Muslims (1961 – 3,034,332 or 7.6% of total population).[17] This is a phenomenal growth in the number of Buddhists in Maharashtra. The figures for other areas populated by the Mahars are also impressive for the growth of Buddhist populations between 1951 and 1961: (Andhra Pradesh, from 230 to 6,753; Madhya Pradesh, from 2,291 to 113,365). Most of the rise in the Buddhist population, it may be validly assumed, came from the conversion of the Mahars to Buddhism in response to Ambedkar's call and action at Nagpur in 1956. The figures for the latest census are not available as of this writing, but it may be safely assumed that the rise over the 1961 figures in the number of Buddhists in Maharashtra and elsewhere cannot be very high as the tempo of the Buddhist conversion movement among the Mahars seems to have visibly slowed down in the absence of Ambedkar's leadership.

Ambedkar's rebellion, on the reckoning shown above, meant a loss of nearly three million followers for Hinduism within a span of a few years. This was easily the most serious challenge faced by Hinduism in recent times and though the rate of conversions has obviously slowed down, the emergence of Mahars as a new Buddhist and minority community in its midst has created problems for Hinduism. The actual impact of such conversions on the status

---

16   For these interpretations see his *The Buddha And His Dhamma* (Bombay, 1957).
17   *Census Of India*, 1961 (Delhi, 1961 ?), I, Pt. II-C(i), pp. 482–483.

of the Mahars living in villages can be gauged only when field surveys are
carried out. But if general indications are any reliable guide, these conversions
have made little difference to their day-to-day lives in rural parts. Tensions
between Mahars converted to Buddhism and caste Hindus, especially of the
Maratha caste, are sporadically reported in the press. The paradox is that
whereas the Brahman seems to have accepted the awakening of the Mahar
and his new status, the dominant Maratha caste seems to have sharpened its
hostility toward the Mahar turned Buddhist in some areas. Ambedkar was
apprehensive of this and expressed his fears in 1955 suggesting that instead of
a single Marathi-speaking state it would be better to create three separate
Marathi-speaking units so that the tyranny of the Marathas – the dominant
caste – over Mahars, as well as Brahmans and others, could be mitigated to
an extent.[18] In countless villages, therefore, things for the untouchables have
not changed much. The one impact of Ambedkar's rebellion has been for the
untouchable to be more aware of his plight and rights and seek, however
timidly, remedial measures through his participation in the electoral process
and the influence of his caste legislators in the state capitals and New Delhi.
There is also a remarkable urge to seek avenues of education, new modes of
employment, and movement toward urban areas. As for the Buddhist movement, it seems to have reached a plateau and the significance and larger
meaning of the conversion process seem to be weakening as time passes.

But Ambedkar's significance as the greatest untouchable rebel against
Hinduism and Hindu society cannot be underestimated either in its form or
effects. Ambedkar accomplished for the untouchables within a few decades
what had remained only a hope for centuries. His life has left an indelible
impression not only on millions of his followers but also on the political and
social movements in modern India. He began his life with a rebellion against
an ancient and strongly established tradition and ended it by a return to another and equally ancient tradition as a means of "modernization" and a
great cultural leap from the "little" tradition to a "great" tradition.

---

18   *Thoughts On Linguistic States* (Aurangabad, 1955), p. 24.

The Izhavas of Kerala and their Historic Struggle* for Acceptance in the Hindu Society

CYRIAc K. PULLAPILLY

Saint Mary's College, Notre Dame, U.S.A.

THERE ARE over six million Izhavas or Thiyas (as they are known in the northern parts) in the state of Kerala. They form nearly one-third of the population of the state and they are the single largest communal group there. They are still listed among the backward communities by the Government of India and the state government, which makes them eligible for some special privileges such as reserved seats and scholarships in colleges and professional schools. They are engaged in all sorts of professions, but large numbers of them are still involved in toddy-tapping or extracting sweet juices from coconut and palm trees which are fermented and sold in liquor shops, so much so that they are as a community still justifiably identified with the toddy and liquor business – their traditional caste occupation.

Since the 1920's at least they have been extremely active socially and politically. Their communal organization, Sri Narayana Dharma Paripalana Yogam, founded in 1903, has since become perhaps the largest and best organized of its kind in the state. Under its aegis the Izhavas operate twelve colleges, several dozen high schools and elementary schools, several hospitals,

* The author is particularly indebted to the following persons, among many others too numerous to mention, for giving their time generously for interviews as well as for their hospitality: R. Sankar, former chief minister of Kerala and presently president of S.N.D.P. Yogam Trust Fund; K. Balarama Panikar, former principal of the Sankrit College and author of the massive Sankrit work on the teachings of Guru Narayana; Murkot Kunhappa, associate editor of *Malayala Manorama*, the leading daily newspaper in Kerala; K. Sukumaran, managing editor of *Keralakoumudi*, the only daily newspaper run by Izhavas; A. Aiyappan, former chancellor of Kerala University and presently director of the Anthropological Institute, Calicut; Nataraja Guru, philosopher and closest disciple of Sri Narayana Guru; P. S. Velayudhan, principal of Sri Narayana College, Quilon; A. R. Achuthan, historian and biographer of *C. Krishnan*; Nijananda Swami, secretary of Sri Narayana Dharma Sangham and head of the monastic order. Murkot Kumhappa, A. R. Achuthan and Nijananda Swami also gave him materials of historical value. He is also grateful to Bhikshu Dharmaskandha, one of the three original Buddhist bhikshus who came from Ceylon in 1935, for sending him many documents concerning the Buddhist movement among Izhavas.

and hundreds of village meeting halls. It also sponsors banks, credit unions, cooperatives, and small scale industries for the benefit of the community. At least one widely circulating daily newspaper and several monthly and weekly periodicals are published by Izhavas. None of them is an official organ of the community, yet they all have a special interest in its welfare. The Izhavas have their own temples and shrines which number in the hundreds. Monastic tradition is rather recent among them, yet they have several monasteries, the most important being the one at Sivagiri, the place of samadhi of Sri Narayana Guru, their most important saint and social reformer.

The Izhavas participated fully in the nationalist movement, and produced some of the foremost political leaders of the region who served in the state's ministries since independence. They have also a representation, proportionate to their number, in the judicial and legislative branches of the state government as well as a similar representation in the central legislature. They patronize all the political parties of the state and all shades of political philosophies are represented among them, but by far the largest number of them belong to one of two factions of the Communist party of Kerala; in fact, they can be considered the mainstay of the party in the state.

The present situation of the Izhava community, then, is quite bright, and they are a socially alive and politically powerful group, despite their backward class status and their persistent complaint of under-representation in government jobs. They are also on an equal footing with the caste Hindus, Christians, and Mohammedans, socially and politically, although they still are not accepted within the caste system of Hinduism. Their condition, however, has not been this good until recently. In fact, their history since Brahminic Hinduism strongly established itself in South India in the eighth century has been a constant struggle for equality with the caste Hindus – which is the central theme of this essay.

I

As the Izhavas are, unlike any other outcaste Hindus, independent of high caste Hindus in their religious worship, with their own temples and priesthood, and because they form an autonomous social group by themselves, the question whether they were indigenous to Kerala was raised by historians. Until recently the prevalent theory was that they migrated from Ceylon.[1] The very names, Izhavas and Thiyas, are brought to support this theory, as they probably derived from the roots of *Izham* and *Dweep* both of which signify island. The long standing legend that the king of Ceylon sent four bachelors to establish

1 I mention only a few of the more important historians who held this view. V. Nagam Aiya, *The Travancore State Manual*, II, (Trivandrum: Travancore Government Press, 1906), 398–402; Edgar Thurston, *Castes and Tribes of India*, II, (Madras: Government Press, 1909), 292–418; William Logan, *Malabar* ("Logan's Manual"), I, (Madras: Government Press, 1951), 116; C. A. Innes, gen. ed., *Madras District Gazateers*, Vol. I: *Malabar*, ed. by F. B. Evans (Madras: Government Press, 1951), 124–25.

coconut farming in Kerala in the first century A.D. at the request of the Chera king Bhaskara Ravi Varma also lends some support to this theory.[2] There might well have been some migrations from Ceylon in the first century, and there certainly were many both ways since then, but this does not explain the introduction of coconut in Kerala as the nut had already become legendary in Kerala as early as the time of the *Ramayana*. The *Kishkindha* and *Sundara kandams* of the *Ramayana* contain references to the coconuts of Kerala, which makes coconut growing at least as old as the first century A.D., or even as old as 1650 B.C., if we were to accept A. Balakrishna Pillai's computation of the time of the composition of the epic.[3] The greatest difficulty about the migration theory is that small scale migrations cannot explain the largeness of the community, nor is there any record or even legend of any large scale migrations. The close affinity of the customs and habits of the Izhavas to those of the Nairs also argues against the migration theory – as we shall see later. The same objections could rule out the theory which explains the origin of Izhavas from Bali island.[4] Yet still another migration theory was advocated by A. Balakrishna Pillai which ties the Izhavas with the ancient Phoenicians who supposedly arrived by sea in the Gujarat and Sind area about 5000 B.C. and who eventually established the Indus valley civilization. According to this theory, the Phoenicians brought the coconut from some South American island to India, spreading the tree on the way all along the South Pacific.[5] If this was the case Izhavas are part of the Dravidian stock which was pushed eastward and southward by the invading Aryans in the second millennium B.C. Hence the ethnic and cultural similarities of the people of the eastern and southern parts of the subcontinent.

At any rate, the prevalent scholarly opinion today is that the Izhavas are descendants of the early Dravidian settlers of Kerala, and that except for the Namboothiri Brahmins who arrived from the north in the eighth century or around that time, the black outcastes such as the Parayas, Pulayas, Ulladas, etc., who were aboriginal tribes in the area, and some of the Syrian Christians who migrated from the Middle East, all other communities of contemporary Kerala descended from the same ethnic stock.[6] There are innumerable simi-

---

2 All the above mentioned historians (note 1) allude to this legend. For a critique of it see K. R. Narayanan, "Izhavar Oru Padhanam," *Vivekodayam*, Special Issue, January 1967, p. 29.

3 For a discussion of the Ramayana references to coconuts see, *ibid.*

4 This theory is based on a philological interpretation of the synonym of Bali, *Sundhi*, from which the term *Saundhikan* was derived, meaning toddy-tapper, and from the similarities of toddy-tapping techniques used by the Izhavas and the Bali islanders.

5 A critique of this theory in K. R. Narayanan, "Izhavar Oru Padhanam," pp. 29–30.

6 E. M. S. Sankaran Namboothiripadu, *Keralam Malayalikalude Mathrubhumi*, Vol. I, (Desabhimani Publishing House, 1947); K. R. Narayanan, "Izhavar Oru Padhanam;" N. R. Krishnan, *Ezhavar Annum Ennum* (Engandiyar: Seena Publications, 1960); Sooranattu Kunjan Pillai, "Keralathinte Ulpathiyum Keralajanathayum," *History on the March*, Proceedings of the History Convention, Ernakulam, 1965 (Ernakulam: Kerala History Association, 1966), pp. 65–70; M. G. S. Narayanan, "The Growth of Aryan Influence in Ancient Kerala," *History on the March*, pp. 55–63; V. V. K. Valath, "Rigve-

larities between the religious and communal customs of these communities which indicate a common heritage. The similarities between the two most numerous of these communities, the Izhavas and the Nairs, are particularly pertinent here. The observance of *Pula* (the taboos and rituals after death in a family), for example, which is common to both communities does indicate a cultural similarity, but the observance of it between aristocratic ancient families of the two communities cannot be explained by anything other than common parentage.[7] The ritual use of *Vannathimattu* (a white sheet laundered by the female members of the Vannan caste) as a symbol of purification after the *pula* (impurity) incurred by death or childbirth in the family is another custom common to not only Izhavas and Nairs but also to Brahmins.[8] Similarities of other taboos and purification rituals of the Nair and Izhava communities connected with death, cremation, childbirth, menstrual periods of women, and like occasions also add weight to the theory of their common heritage.[9] Common matrilineal tradition is still another indication of the ethnic identity of the two communities.[10] Isolated cases in northern Kerala of Nairs still serving as best men for Izhava weddings show that they consider each other as cousins.[11] So also does the north Malabar custom of Nair girls addressing Izhava women as *ammalu akkan*, meaning older sister.[12] Still another very important similarity of the two communities is their martial tradition. The Nairs are generally accepted as the martial class of Kerala, although they are accorded only a *shudra* status in the caste structure. But folklore, tradition, and written records show that the Izhavas have also been a martial class. The folk songs, *Vadakkan Pattukal*, composed about four hundred years ago are full of descriptions of the military exploits of Izhava heroes.[13] And there is no doubt that the Izhavas served in the armed forces of all the important kings of the region, such as the Zamorins of Calicut and the kings of Travancore and Cochin. Their martial identity is so well recognized that *chekon*, a derivation of *sevakan*, meaning soldier, became their vulgarized communal title.[14]

The above arguments indicate the ethnic identity of the Izhavas with at

dakalathe Keralam," *History on the March*, pp. 121–125; K. Balarama Panikar, a private interview held, Trivandrum, July 1971; R. Sankar, a private interview held, Quilon, August 1971.

7 Many such instances are recorded by the following authors. K. Ananthan, *Keralacharithranirupanam* (Cannanore: Edwards Press, 1935), pp. 85–97; K. R. Narayanan, "Izhavar Oru Padhanam," pp. 30–31.

8 Murkot Kumaran, et. al., *Achannu Sesham* (Tellisserry: Kerala Printing and Publishing Company, 1950), pp. 14–20; K. Ananthan, *Keralacharithranirupanam*, pp. 85–97; K. R. Narayanan, "Izhavar Oru Padhanam, pp. 30–31.

9 Logan's Manual, pp. 144–45; sources in note 8.

10 *Ibid.*

11 K. R. Narayanan, "Izhavar Oru Padhanam," p. 31.

12 *Ibid.*

13 *24 Vadakkan Pattukal* (Quilon: Sri Rama Vilasam Press, 1967). Especially the songs "Aromal Chekavar" (pp. 128–148), "Valia Aromal Chekavar" (pp. 148–206), and "Thacholli Othenan" (pp. 283–308).

14 K. R. Narayanan, "Izhavar Oru Padhanam," pp. 31–32.

least the other most numerous Hindu community of Kerala, the Nairs. How then did the Izhavas become outcastes while their cousins, the Nairs, received a place in the Hindu caste structure, at least as the lowest caste, the *shudras*? One theory holds that this development occurred when the Aryan Jains introduced caste distinction in Kerala prior to the eighth century A.D., but only on an occupational basis.[15] The Aryans upon their arrival in Kerala needed protection, for which they selected a group of local sympathizers who were given *kshatriya* functions, but only *shudra* status. Thus originated the Nairs. The rest of the population, including the islanders or planters of coconuts (obviously Izhavas), became outcastes. The other theory holds that it was the Namboothiri Brahmins who introduced the caste system in Kerala in the eighth century or thereabouts.[16] According to this theory, when the Namboothiris arrived in Kerala the civilized population of the area (as opposed to the aboriginal tribes) had become Buddhists through the influence of missionaries who came from the north by land or by sea from Ceylon.[17] The Namboothiris started to arrive in Kerala in considerable numbers during the period of Brahminic revival, inaugurated by Sri Sankaracharya (788–820) and continued by Kumarilabhattan, Sambandhamoorthi, Parasuraman, and many others. Brahminic influence in South India dated as far back as the first century A.D. as there are numerous mentions of it in the Tamil Sangham literature of between the first and the fourth centuries of the Christian era.[18] Their strong influence on Kerala proper, however, must be dated much later, probably coincidental with the development of Kerala as a cultural region separate from the old Tamilakam or Tamil region and Malayalam as a separate language. This occurred anywhere from the seventh to the tenth centuries as the Aryan influx reached a climax due to the favorable political conditions under patronage of invading Aryan princes or local rulers whom the Brahmins served as counsellors, ministers, and priests. The legendary creation of Kerala by Parasuraman, probably an Aryan prince from Malwar, by throwing an ax into the Arabian sea and thereby making the water to recede (the recession of the sea from much of the western coast of Kerala around this time is un-questionable, whatever its cause may have been) may have occurred around this time.[19] In any case, Namboothiri Brahmins were able to infiltrate Kerala

---

15   William Logan, *Malabar*, 155 ff.: V. T. Induchoodan, "Koodalmanikakshetravum Kera-lacharitravum," *Vivekodayam*, Sivagirithirthadanam Supplement, 1970, pp. 251–54.

16   E. M. S. Sankaran Namboothiripadu, *Keralam*, pp. 39–47; R. Sankar, interview; K. Balarama Panikar, interview; K. R. Narayanan, "Izhavar Oru Padhanam," p. 31 and in "Chathurvarnyam: Jathivyavastha," *Sri Narayana Guru Souvenir* (Sivagiri, 1967), pp. 151–58.

17   For concise studies of Buddhism in Kerala see Velayudhan Panikkasseri, "Budhamatham Keralathil," *Vivekodayam*, Special issue, September 1968, pp. 131–37; S. Sanku Iyar, "Budhakalaghattam Keralathil," *History on the March*, pp. 151–58.

18   M. G. S. Narayanan, "The Growth of Arian (sic) Influence in Ancient Kerala," *History on the March*, pp. 56–57.

19   *Ibid.*, pp. 56–61; K. K. Pillay, "Aryan Influence in Kerala History," *ibid.*, pp. 137–50.

successfully around this time and completely revamp the religious, social, political, and economic structure of the area.

Religiously, they replaced Buddhism with Brahminic Hinduism by destroying Buddhist temples and monasteries or transforming them into Hindu temples.[20] Whatever Buddhist temples remained unmolested by the Brahmins, for one reason or another, eventually became temples of pre-Aryan gods and goddesses such as Durga, Kali, Bhagavati, and the like. This was only a natural outcome of the situation as the Brahmins effectively destroyed the leadership of the new religion by abolishing Buddhist monasteries and learning centers.[21] K. Balarama Panikar argues that the Brahmins introduced even animal sacrifices and vulgar festivities such as the *pooram pattu*[22] in old Buddhist temples in order to drive away Buddhist monks and devotees.[23] Thus eventually these temples became centers of worship for that part of the civilized population of Kerala which did not readily accept Brahminic Hinduism, where worship of pre-Aryan local gods and goddesses was reintroduced.

Socially, they effected a complete transformation in Kerala in various ways. Introduction of the caste system was one. The Namboothiris set themselves up as the highest caste while accepting that part of the population which cooperated with them within the system as the lowest caste, the *shudras*.[24] They set up cooperating local rulers as *kshatriyas*.[25] This perhaps may explain why there are so few *kshatriyas* in Kerala and no *vaishyas* at all to speak of and such large numbers of *shudras*. Another major social innovation of the Namboothiris in Kerala was the matrilineal system, which they introduced in order to insure that their family properties would not change hands.[26] So was the custom of *sambandham* or union between a Namboothiri and a *shudra* woman, not really a marriage as it did not involve any legal inheritance from the father. It was only a provision for the sons of the Namboothiris, other than the first who inherited the family property, to have families but with no concomitant responsibility. The raising of children was largely the woman's responsibility under this system, although the Namboothiris often made some provisions for their progenies in varying degrees.[27]

Economically, the Namboothiris seem to have established themselves as the landlords of Kerala between the ninth and eleventh centuries. Legends of local rulers inviting Brahmins from the north, providing them with extensive

---

20 *Ibid.*, S. Sanku Iyar, "Budhakalaghattam Keralathil," pp. 151–58.
21 *Ibid.*, E. M. S. Sankaran Namboothiripadu, Keralam, p. 39.
22 A singing, dancing ceremony where the participants shout vulgarities and sometimes indulge in sensual gestures and activities.
23 Interview.
24 M. G. S. Narayanan, "The Growth of Arian (sic) Influence in Ancient Kerala," pp. 61–62; K. Ananthan, *Keralacharithranirupanam*, pp. 81–8; R. Sankar, interview; K. Balarama Panikar, interview.
25 M. G. S. Narayanan, "The Growth of Arian (sic) Influence in Ancient Kerala," pp. 57–58.
26 *Ibid.*, K. K. Pillay, "Aryan Influence in Kerala History," pp. 137–50.
27 K. K. Pillay, "Aryan Influence...," pp. 144–45.

land holdings, and of Namboothiris colonizing under the protection of various royal patrons, especially under the Chalukya rulers, abound during this period.[28] The most important of them, of course, is that of Parasuraman himself, who after his miraculous creation of Kerala, donated the new land to Brahmins of thirty-two families.[29] This legend also has its origin about the same time or a little after the vast majority of the land holdings of Kerala had come into the possession of the Namboothiris either directly or indirectly through the temples which they controlled. At any rate, by the eleventh century A.D. much of the arable land of Kerala was under the control of the Namboothiri Brahmins, a situation which remained unchanged until recent times. Only under the unsettling conditions after Tipu Sultan's invasion of Kerala in the closing years of the eighteenth century did the Brahminic domination of landed properties begin to change.[30]

Culturally, too, the Namboothiri Brahmins effected a complete transformation of Kerala, introducing Sanskrit and Sanskrit literature there and eventually developing the Malayalam language and literature in the region blending Sanskrit and the indigenous Tamil.[31]

It seems certain that by the close of the first millennium A.D. the Brahmins had achieved prominence in the economic, social, cultural and religious milieu of Kerala. That they achieved this at the expense of the Buddhist believers is evidenced by, among other things, the presence of numerous ruined Buddhist temples, many of them yet to be unearthed by archaeologists, in Kerala and the cultural mores that attach a stigma to things Buddhist, as indicated by the term, *boudha*, which literally means Buddhist but in the vulgar terminology is a synonym for idiot. That the Izhavas had been staunch Buddhists, and thus were constrained to constitute themselves as an outcaste society under Brahminic domination, may be substantiated by their still prevalent non-ritualistic and non-dogmatic character and their emphasis on the moral aspects of religion rather than the theological, which are qualities generally attributed to Buddhism. For example, they have never been noted for their temple-going and participation in religious rituals. Even when they agitated for the right to enter state-owned Hindu temples[32] they did so as a matter of basic human

---

28 M. G. S. Narayanan, "The Growth of Arian (sic) Influence...," pp. 58–60.
29 *Ibid.*, K. K. Pillay, "Aryan Influence...," pp. 143–44.
30 K. K. Pillay, "Aryan Influence...," p. 144.
31 P. K. Parameswaran Nair, *Malayala Sachithya Charithram* (New Delhi: Sahithya Academy, 1969), pp. 18–20; K. K. Pillay, "Aryan Influence...," pp. 147–50.
32 There were numerous agitations for temple-entry rights by low castes, mainly by Izhavas, the most famous of them being the 1924 Vaikom Satyagraha in which Gandhi participated and the large scale demonstrations of the 1930's in Travancore and Cochin states. The latter resulted in the Temple Entry Proclamation of 1936 by the King of Travancore, which opened state-owned temples to all Hindus. The following references are representative of a very large amount of literature available on the subject. C. V. Kunjuraman, "Njangalkum Sirkar Kshetrangalil Onnu," an editorial in *Desabhimani* of 1918, reproduced in *Vivekodayam*, Special Issue, January 1967, pp. 173–74; K. R. Narayanan, "Vaikathu Nadannittulla Aithochadanasramangal—Oru Thirinjunottam," *Vivedkodayam*, special issue, Sept. 1968, pp. 185–191; M. C. Joseph, "Kshetrapravesanam," *ibid.*, pp. 103–106;

right and as a way of getting accepted in the Hindu society rather than from any great desire to go to the temples. In fact, some Izhavas agitated for rejection of temples at the same time their brothers agitated for the right to enter the temples. Their emphasis on the moral as opposed to the theological and ritualistic aspects of religion is epitomized by the only religious concept that had a distinctly Izhava origin, that is the *advaita* or non-dualistic principle as enunciated by Sri Narayana Guru, the practical expression of which is capsuled in two slogans: "one caste, one religion, one God" and "whatever be man's religion it is enough that he be good."[33] The preponderance of Izhavas among Ayurveda physicians, a medical discipline which has distinctly Buddhistic origins, and among astrologers, also a discipline which had grown significantly in Buddhist India, is still another argument often advanced in support of the Buddhist past of the Izhavas.[34] Statistics about the percentage of Izhavas among Ayurvedic physicians and astrologers are not readily available but it is unquestionable that their numbers are disproportionately large.

It is then a plausible theory that the Izhavas had been Buddhists, and that under the socio-cultural and religious milieu of a resurgent Brahminism they gradually lost their identity, having been cut off from the sustaining sources of Buddhism, namely its shrines, temples, and monasteries – much the same as what happened to Buddhism in its other last Indian stronghold, Bengal.[35] In the case of the Izhavas, however, they not only lost their religious identity but they were also relegated to an outcaste status and by and large they also lost their property and civil rights.[36] It seems that as a result of discriminatory treatment at the hands of the Brahmin-dominated Hindu society over many centuries they eventually acquiesced in their outcaste and non-privileged status, having taken up toddy-tapping as a means of livelihood for the most part and having returned to their pre-Buddhist local gods for religious worship. It was not until the second half of the nineteenth century that they launched any large scale agitation to regain their long lost rights. Although their continued collaboration with their erstwhile cousins, the Nairs, in social, communal and ritualistic practices[37] and although the continued presence of many Izhava

M. Prabha, "C.V. and Kshetrapravesanavilambaram," *Vivekodayam*, C.V. Kunjuraman Birth Centenary Supplement, April 1971, pp. 59–62; C. O. Karunakaran, "The Temple Entry Proclamation," *S.N.D.P. Yogam Golden Jubilee Souvenir* (Quilon, 1953), pp. 109–110; two statements by Sirdar K. M. Panikkar, one in his autobiography and the other in his forward to the life of T. K. Madhavan, both included in P. K. Balakrishnan, ed., *Narayanaguru Samagraha Grandham* (Kottayam: National Book Stall, 1969), pp. 96–97.

33   For the above I follow R. Sankar and K. Balarama Panikar. Interview.

34   *Ibid.*, Bhikshu Dharmaskandhan, "Ayurveda Vaidynmar," *Mahabodhi Souvenir* (Calicut, 1964), pp. 99–101.

35   See note no. 20.

36   See notes nos. 21, 22, 23; Velayudhan Panikkassery, "Budhamatham Keralathil," *Vivekodayam*, Special Issue, Sept. 1968, pp. 131–137; and for a general treatise on the ruins of Buddhist temples, V. K. Parameswaren Pillai, "Keralavum Budhamathavum," *Mahabodhi Upaharagrandham*, Dr. *V.I. Raman Souvenir* (Calicut, 1951), pp. 25–27.

37   See notes 7–14.

royal families such as the Mannanar dynasty of Malabar,[38] who maintained their royal status if not their Buddhist heritage even after the Brahminization of Kerala, constantly reminded the Izhavas of their past prominence, they were by and large too disorganized and incapacitated to do anything about their condition except for occasional small scale attempts to enter Hindu temples and other protests. In the nineteenth century, however, a new element which was introduced into Kerala society, namely the presence of large numbers of Westerners, proved to be a stimulant to various sorts of movements for social reform, including the Izhavas.

II

The influence of Western missionaries has been most notable in this regard. Portuguese missionaries who followed St. Francis Xavier had converted to Catholicism large numbers of low castes, including some Izhavas, on the western shores of Kerala. But the large scale influx of Western missionaries, especially Protestant, in the aftermath of the evangelical movements of the nineteenth century had a substantial influence on the lower classes of Kerala. Apart from their proselytization, they also provided educational opportunities, and introduced their followers to Christian moral values, which proved to be a catalyst for social change.[39] The Nadar Rebellion of 1858 is a case in point. The main focus of the rebellion was the right of Nadar women to cover their breasts, which had been forbidden by state law not only for Nadars but also for their cousins and fellow toddy-tappers, the Izhavas, and all other outcastes. Guided by motives of Christian modesty, the missionaries demanded, with the rebellious support in this case of the Nadars of South Travancore, that the low caste women be permitted to wear "uppercloths."[40] After several years of rebellion on the part of the Nadars and violent repression on the part of the caste Hindus, especially the Nairs, it was the direct intervention of the British Governor of Madras that brought about the two proclamations from the kings of Travancore, one in 1859 (Kollam Era 1034) by Maharaja Utram Thirunal and the other in 1865 (Kollam Era 1040) by Maharaja Ayilyam Thirunal, abolishing the restrictions concerning "uppercloths."[41] If the Nadars of South Travancore, who were in large part converted to Christianity, agitated for causes related to typically Christian concerns, their fellow toddy-tappers, the Izhavas, found causes closely related to their own past history, such as the right to enter public temples along with caste Hindus. Numerous agitations

38 Kampil Ananthan, "Mannanar Oru Purathana Rajavamsam," *Cochin S.N.D.P. Souvenir,* 1946. I am indebted to the courtesy of Prof. K. R. Achuthan who was kind enough to send me a handwritten copy of this article.

39 M. O. Joseph, "Keralavum Christian Missionarimarum," *History on the March,* pp. 159–166.

40 K. Kochukrishnan Nadar, *Nadar Charithram* (Kanjiramkulam: Desabhimani Publishing House, 1956), pp. 186–198.

41 *Ibid.*

were conducted, some of them violent which were repressed with even more violence by caste Hindus,[42] the culmination of which was the famous Vaikom Satyagraham of 1924 in which Mahatma Gandhi participated. The Temple Entry Proclamation of 1936 by the king of Travancore, which opened state-owned temples to non-caste Hindus, was a result of this.[43] Travancore and the other previous states of Kerala were not the only scenes of temple-entry agitations but the whole of South India where large numbers of people had been disenfranchised religiously and civilly since the Brahminic domination. The Temple Entry Authorization and Indemnity Act of 1939 passed by the Madras legislature under the Congress government of Chief Minister C. Rajagopalachari was a result of such agitations in Tamilnad.[44]

Temple entry was only one of the issues in which the Izhavas were interested. Numerous other issues concerning civil rights and a fair share of government jobs and of the region's wealth also attracted their attention. But active agitation concerning these causes presupposed a certain amount of social consciousness and educational preparation on the part of at least a good number of Izhavas, which did not become a reality until the early part of the twentieth century. It was the educational and economic opportunities provided by the British in the province of Malabar in northern Kerala that made a difference in this regard.

Unlike their cousins to the south in the states of Travancore and Cochin who continued to suffer discriminatory treatment under the Hindu kings, the Izhavas of Malabar, who are known by the name of Thiyas and sometimes claim different ethnic origins, enjoyed equal treatment under the British rule ever since the English had taken control of the area in the 1790's in the aftermath of the war with Tipu and finally had annexed the whole region to the Madras Presidency in 1800. Indeed, the Thiyas received even special treatment as their community was the only one that was flexible enough to mingle freely with the English and to take full advantage of all the educational and economic opportunities provided by them. The historic estrangement of the Thiyas/Izhavas from the mainstream of caste Hindu society seems to be the main reason for this development.

Perhaps an exceptional kind of Thiya collaboration with the English, but one that provoked the indignation of the elders was the mixing of many Thiya women with the officers and soldiers of the British battalion stationed in Cannanore since the early nineteenth century. The numbers of Thiya women

---

42 Records of such temple entry agitations, which were frequent occurrences even before the time of Christian missionaries, are extremely scant. A brief treatise on some of those agitations which occurred in and around the famous temple of Vaikom since 1700 is available in K. R. Narayanan, "Vaikathu Nadannittulla Ayithochadanasramangal...," pp. 185–191. More on the famous 1924 demonstrations, K. P. Kesava Menon, "Satyagrahasmaranakal," *S.N.D.P. Yogam Golden Jubilee Souvenir*, pp. 91–92.
43 See note 32.
44 Robert L. Hardgrave, Jr., *The Nadars of Tamilnad, The Political Culture of a Community in Change* (Berkeley and Los Angeles: University of California Press, 1969), p. 188.

associated with English men, mostly as concubines and in some cases as wives, was not very large but in several generations at least a small portion of the Thiya community had varying amounts of European blood in them, enough to result in different degrees of change in their pigmentation and physical features. What started as the erratic behavior of some greedy women, which at least once provoked official condemnation and the excommunication of the aberrants by the elders of the community,[45] eventually became an accepted practice as the progeny of these unions received better education than the rest of the community, and consequently obtained important jobs and social prominence under the British regime. Indeed, within the space of a few generations the lighter skinned progeny of mixed unions were not only accepted in orthodox Thiya society but they even were held in high esteem, and intermarriage with their children became fashionable.[46] The end result of all this was a generally well-educated Thiya community, enjoying special privileges under their British protectors, so much so that practically all the Indian-born higher officers in the administration of the province until the second quarter of the twentieth century came from the Thiya community.[47]

The Thiyas also took full advantage of the social and economic reforms administered by the British, an example of which was their exploitation of the new excise regulations which made the production and distribution of toddy and other alcoholic beverages a profitable enterprise both for the industry and the government. Indeed, by reasons of their history, Thiyas became the monopolists in the liquor industry.[48] Their progress in commerce and agriculture was also notable at this period. They were still outcastes before the Hindu caste society, however, in stark contrast to the tremendous social and economic improvements they had made. Some sort of agitation for reform of the Hindu caste system, then, was inevitable in Malabar.

The Izhavas of the southern princely states of Kerala also were beneficiaries of similar socio-economic changes, although in a much lesser degree, as the Rajas of Travancore and Cochin also instituted many reforms, either dictated by their British Residents or pressed upon them by popular sentiment, the Nadar rebellion being a case in point. As a result of these developments, the Izhava/Thiya community had attained, by the first quarter of the twentieth century, a level of social consciousness, identity, and ambition, enough to launch large scale agitations for the removal of the many inequalities they had been victims of since the Brahminic domination of the ninth century A.D.

Paramount among these inequalities was their outcaste status, upon which

45 Murkot Kumaran, et. al., *Achannu Sesham*, p. 26.
46 For the above I am indebted to Mr. Murkot Kunhappa, associate editor of *Malayalama-norama* and a prominent figure in the Thiya community, for sending me a lengthy manuscript treatise on this matter, especially prepared for me from his own family papers and from the unpublished writings of his father, Murkot Kumaran.
47 Murkot Kumaran, *Achannu Sesham*, p. 27; Murkot Kunhappa, unpublished manuscript (note 46); O. Abu, "Sriman Churayil Kamaran," *S.N.D.P. Yogam Golden Jubilee Souvenir* pp. 245–48; M. C. Govindan, "C. Krishnan," *ibid.*, pp. 43–44.
48 Murkot Kumaran, *Achannu Sesham*, pp. 30–31.

all social and economic discriminations against them were founded. The right
to enter temples, especially those state-owned temples which they also supported with their taxes, had, therefore, a central and symbolic significance.
It was indeed to this right that their early demonstrations were dedicated.[49]
If temple entry was such a crucial issue for the Izhavas, and thus vigorously
pursued, it was equally important for the caste Hindus to refuse them this
right. Thus the resistance was as vigorous as the agitations. By the first quarter
of the twentieth century, then, it was clear that no progress could be made on
this issue unless a drastic change occurred in the Hindu hierarchical structure
of Kerala, which was virtually impossible. By then the Izhava/Thiya community also had attained a sociological maturity and had developed enough
leadership to look at alternate solutions for their ills. The religious question
continued to be their central concern, however. It could not have been otherwise in the cultural milieu of Kerala.

III

The most important of the many courses of action undertaken by the
Izhava community for the amelioration of their condition was the one guided
by Sri Narayana Guru, prophet and social reformer. The Guru was born
probably in 1854 in Chempazhanthi, a village not too far from the state capital
of Trivandrum. His life until 1887, the year in which his public life began with
the symbolic consecration of a Shiva shrine, lies buried in numerous legends
and myths.[50] It is generally accepted, however, that he spent his early years
in his native village, received some amount of literary and religious education
from a Nair guru of a neighboring village, and taught Sanskrit and religion to
children of his own and a neighboring village, for some years.[51] It is quite
probable, too, that he led a married life for a few years, although his worshipful
biographers ignored this part of his life out of reverence for his later asceti-
cism.[52] It is also probable that he attained a great degree of yoga discipline
and contemplation with the inspiration of several friends and colleagues,
notably Chattampi Swami and Thykkad Ayyavu, two prominent ascetics of
the time, and that he spent several years as an itinerant yogi in several parts
of Kerala, including the hills of Cape Comerin, the legendary abode of
gods.[53] By 1887 he was widely known as a learned guru and saintly yogi and

49 See the sources in note no. 32; K. Aiyappan, "Keralathile Samudayaparishkaram,"
    S.N.D.P. Yogam Golden Jubilee Souvenir, pp. 79–80.
50 Sukumaran Pottakatt, "Aruvippuram Prathishtakku Munpu," *Sri Narayana Guru Cen-
    tenary Souvenir* (Varkala, 1954), pp. 35–37; N. R. Krishnan, "Sri Narayana Guruvum
    Sri Chattampi Swamikalum," *ibid.,* pp. 150–164.
51 Nataraja Guru, *The Word of the Guru* (Ernakulam: Paico Publishing House, 1968), p. 256.
52 P. K. Balakrishnan, "Jivithathile Oru Prasnam," P. K. Balakrishnan, ed., Narayana
    Guru Samahara Grandham (Kottayam: National Book Stall, 1969), pp. 134–40; Nata-
    raja Guru, *The Word of the Guru,* pp. 260–61.
53 N. R. Krishnan, "Sri Narayana Guruvum Sri Chattampi Swamikalum," pp. 150–64;
    Nataraja Guru, *The Word of the Guru,* pp. 257–60.

was deeply revered among his own Izhava community. His consecration of a
Shiva shrine in that year at Aruvippuram was, therefore, widely noticed.

The shocking unorthodoxy of this act was the main reason it received such
wide attention, for no non-Brahmin had the right to consecrate a god's image
in a temple; indeed, none had ever done so. The inevitably furious reaction
of caste Hindus was countered by the Guru's sarcastic explanation that he
consecrated "only an Izhava Shiva."[54] Apart from being an utterly unorthodox
act, it symbolically and really started a new tradition in which Izhavas once
again had their own priests and places of worship instead of the humiliation
of having to worship from the prescribed outer peripheries of caste Hindu
temples – something they had been fighting against for many centuries. From
1887 until his death in 1928, the Guru and his disciples established so many
temples in all parts of Kerala that by then Izhavas everywhere had their own
temples.

Establishing their own temples for Izhavas was only an aspect of the Guru's
total plan of reform. His primary concern was to eliminate the very system
that denied the right of entering temples to Izhavas and other outcaste Hindus,
the caste system. His inscription on his first temple indicated his intent: "This
is the ideal place where everyone lives in brotherhood, without distinction of
caste and religion."[55] In order to provide philosophical and theological
justification for his casteless society he also developed a theological system, the
advaita (non-dualist) system, which paradoxically enough was a sociological
reinterpretation of the famous theological system of the same name of Shri
Shankara, the ninth century pioneer of Brahminization.[56] The essence and
ultimate conclusion of the Guru's philosophy is oneness, verbalized in his
famous slogan: "One caste, one religion, one God," which is today boldly
inscribed on every Izhava temple, shrine, school and office.

Undergirding his scheme of reform with a philosophical and theological
system that was derived from the most authentic orthodox sources, that is from
Shankara's own works and elaborating on it in nearly four dozen books,
religious tracts, poems and odes written in Sanskrit, Malayalam, and Tamil,[57]
the Guru launched his campaign for reform toward the close of the nineteenth
century. Despite the adamant position of a small group of his disciples under
the leadership of Nataraja Guru (the aged theoretician who considered that
the mantle of the Guru had fallen on him, that Sri Narayana Guru was purely
a religious philosopher who never intended any type of social action, and that

54 Anonymous, "Nalu Prathishtakal," *Vivekodayam*, Special Issue, January 1967, p. 202;
    N. R. Krishnan, "Sri Narayana Guruvum Sri Chattampi Swamikalum," pp. 150–64.
    This episode is also treated in all the biographies of the Guru and in numerous other
    publications concerning him.

55 P. K. Balakrishnan, "Narayana Guru Oru Padhanam," *Narayana Guru Samahara Grand-
    ham*, p. 120.

56 For a comparative study of the *advaita* principles of Sankara and Narayana Guru see
    K. Balarama Panikar, "Advaitham," *S.N.D.P. Yogam Golden Jubilee Souvenir*, pp. 5–8, 46.

57 A complete list of the Guru's works in chronological order of composition in Nataraja
    Guru, *The Word of the Guru*, pp. 389–91.

it was by almost criminal trickery and connivance that the activists of the Izhava community, most prominent of whom was his own father, Dr. Palpu, exploited the fame and saintly aura of the Guru to launch their own plan of social reform),[58] it is clear from the biography of the Guru that he indeed was an astute social reformer and activist.[59] In fact, his plan of social reform was extremely well thought out and systematically organized to touch all the weaknesses of the Izhava society, as evidenced by the plan of action he laid out in 1905 (Kollam Era 1080) for the campaigners of his social organization, the Sri Narayana Dharma Paripalana Yogam, commonly known as the S.N.D.P. Yogam. This plan included four major areas of action: 1. *Religion* – elimination of superstitions, blood sacrifices, and worship of evil gods; fostering of pure Hindu worship and morals; promotion of temples and monasteries wherever they are needed, without causing hardship for people of other religions. 2. *Moral behavior* – promotion of honesty, cleanliness, fear of injustice, nobility, and friendliness; elimination of meaningless old customs and promotion of good timely customs according to the teachings of the Guru. 3. *Education* – a massive re-education of the Izhava community on the usefulness of schooling and the evils of ignorance, with a goal that in the future there will not be any man or woman in the community without at least an elementary education; building of schools and libraries by the community. 4. *Industry* – advancement of agriculture, commerce and small industries; encouragement of frugality; stimulation of the community that laziness and parasitism will be considered anti-social; establishment of factories and technical schools.

Indeed, the Guru's plan of action was so broad, and his saintliness so universally accepted, that every leader of the Izhava community identified himself with the Guru and his plan, whatever his particular area of interest may have been. It was inevitable, then, that an organization of the Izhava community be established, which indeed occurred with the foundation of the S.N.D.P. Yogam in 1903, under the patronage of the Guru and bearing his name. The literal meaning of its title is: the organization dedicated to the promotion of Sri Narayana Guru's philosophy. S.N.D.P. Yogam thus became the forum for Izhava leaders of divergent occupations and interests such as Dr. Palpu, a physician whose major concern was civil rights and equal employment;[60] Kumaran Asan, the poet laureate whose main interest naturally was cultural improvement;[61] C. Krishnan, advocate, banker, publisher, and phi-

---

58 Nataraja Guru, a private interview, Gurukulam Varkala, August 1971.
59 Sri Narayana Guru, "Enthu Pracharippikanam," *Sri Narayana Guru Samaharagrandham*, p. 162; Sri Narayana Guru, "Message to the Annual Meeting of the S.N.D.P. Yogam, 1908," *Vivekodayam*, Special Issue, January 1967, p. 169; C. R. Kesavan Vaidyar, "Vyavasaya Purogathi Sri Narayana Guruvinte Veekshanathil," *Vivekodayam*, Sivagiri Thirthadanam Supplement, 1970, pp. 9-12; V. Jagannatha Panikar, "Gurudeva Chinthayile Dhanathathwadarsanam," *Sri Narayana Guru Souvenir* (Varkala, 1967), pp. 231–32.
60 K. Bhanu, "Dr. Palpu, D. P. H.," *S.N.D.P. Yogam Golden Jubilee Souvenir*, pp. 27–29.
61 K. Sadasivan, "Kumaran Asan," *ibid.*, pp. 35–36, 62–64; M. K. Sanu, "Asan Samudaya Parishkarthavu," *Vivekodayam*, Sri Narayana Guru Souvenir, 1967, pp. 51–55; N. Kumaran Asan, "Samudayathe Parishkarikunnathinu Sakthamaya Oru Vagindriyam,"

lanthropist who, strangely enough, took a special interest in religion and eventually became a Buddhist;[62] T. K. Madhavan, journalist, revolutionary and civil rights activist;[63] Murkot Kumaran, educator and advocate of collective action by all the outcastes;[64] C. V. Kunjuraman, publisher, social critic, and ultimate satirist;[65] "Sahodaran" Ayyappan, advocate of intercaste relations and ultimate unity of castes;[66] and many others of lesser stature.

Yet, despite the universal acceptance of the Guru by all Hindus of Kerala, in fact by all of India, as a major saint and teacher of Hinduism,[67] and despite the unique stature he enjoyed among the Izhavas, as their saint and the architect of their future, his idealistic concept of a casteless society remained just that, a concept. On the one hand the caste Hindus could not stomach such a revolutionary idea, and on the other the Izhavas themselves, who even as outcastes held a higher status than the rest of the outcastes, were unwilling to mingle with those beneath them. The Guru's own personal example of mixing with the lower outcastes, and the efforts of a few idealists such as "Sahodaran" Ayyappan who advocated intercaste relations, did not have any real impact on a caste conscious society. Thus rejecting, for all practical purposes, the basic philosophy of the Guru, the S.N.D.P. Yogam almost from the start emerged as a communal organization of the Izhavas, concerned with their

reprinted in *Vivekodayam*, Special Issue, January 1967, pp. 181–88; N. Kumaran Asan, "Jathi Sankadam," a reprint from his own journal *Mithavadi* of 1917 in *Mahabodhi Budha Mission Souvenir* (Calicut, 1964), pp. 12–18.

62 A. C. Govindan, "C. Krishnan," *S.N.D.P. Yogam Golden Jubilee Souvenir*, pp. 43–44, 55; K. R. Achuthan, *C. Krishnan* (Kottayam: National Book Stall, 1971); C. V. Kunjuraman, *Budha Matha Pradeepam* (No place, publisher or date as the title pages are missing from my copy), pp. 119–156; K. R. Achuthan, "Gurudevanum C. Krishnanum," *Sri Narayana Guru Centenary Souvenir* (Varkala, 1954), pp. 184–86.

63 K. R. Narayanan, "Sri T. K. Madhavan," *S.N.D.P. Yogam Golden Jubilee Souvenir*, pp. 103–104, 204–206, 222–223; T. K. Madhavan, "Vazhi Kooduthal Marunthorum," reprint of a 1918 editorial in his own journal *Desabhimani* in *Vivekodayam*, Special Issue, 1967, pp. 172–74; C. O. Kesavan, "Sri T. K. Madhavanum Swamithruppadangalum," *Sri Narayana Guru Centenary Souvenir*, pp. 176–83.

64 Murkot Kumaran, et. al., *Achannu Sesham*; Parasuraman, "Murkot Kumaran," *S.N.D.P. Yogam Golden Jubilee Souvenir*, pp. 113–114; Murkot Kumaran, unpublished manuscript of a speech delivered at Tellicherry at a Thiya Maha Sabha meeting around 1935; by courtesy of his son Murkot Kunhappa; V. C. Appu Vaidyan, "Gurudevanum Murkot Kumaranum," *Sri Narayana Guru Centenary Souvenir*, pp. 187–89.

65 K. Srinivasan, "C. V. Kunjuraman," *S.N.D.P. Yogam Golden Jubilee Souvenir*, pp. 125–28, 132; V. K. Ammunni, "Samudayatheppatti C. V.," *Vivekodayam*, July 1971, pp. 23–25; C. V. Kunjuraman, "Njangalkum Sirkar Kshetrangalil Onnu," an editorial he wrote for *Desabhimani* in 1918, reprinted in *Vivekodayam*, Special Issue, 1967, pp. 173–74; T. H. P. Chentharasseri, "C. V. Charithradrushtiyil," *Vivekodayam*, April 1971, pp. 53–54; M. Prabha, "C.V. and Kshetrapravesana Vilambaram," *ibid.*, pp. 59–62; C. V. Kunjuraman, "Njan Namboothiri Ayalo," an article published in the weekly *Unni Namboothiri* on an unidentified date, reprinted in *ibid.*, pp. 75–80.

66 T. C. Gopalan, "'Sahodaran' Ayyappan," *Vivekodayam*, July 1971, pp. 181–83.

67 This is evidenced by the reverence exhibited to the Guru by the religious and political leaders of India. See *Sree Narayana Guru Souvenir* (Varkala: Sree Narayana Dharmasangham Trust, 1964).

social and political welfare, as evidenced by the statutes and regulations of the organization and its component societies.[68] The Guru's philosophical concerns and his interest in reformed religious worship also found concrete expression in two groups of followers, the former in the Gurukulam group under Nataraja Guru which promotes Sri Narayana's philosophical teachings through two periodicals, occasional books, and several retreats frequented by young European devotees, and the latter in the more formally organized monastic group called the Sri Narayana Dharma Sangham which oversees Izhava temples and religious services, and which lately established a training center for Izhava priests at its headquarters at Sivagiri, the Guru's place of samadhi. Yet the S.N.D.P. Yogam and its program of social action is the part of the Guru's legacy that more Izhavas identify themselves with actively, as his *advaita* philosophy is largely incomprehensible to ordinary men and as his temples have, in large part, lost their attraction for educated Izhavas for they have become, by and large, imitations of caste Hindu temples where superstitions prevail. The recent elevation of the Guru himself as a god with appropriate worship services for him, especially at Sivagiri, is a case in point. Many Izhavas consider this contrary to the Guru's own wishes as, in their view, he built temples only as a stopgap measure to lure Izhavas away from caste Hindu temples where they practiced superstitions despite the humiliations they suffered there. They point to the fact that it was just a mirror that the Guru dedicated in the last temple he founded, which, according to them, was the culmination of a progressive departure from images and temples – the mirror showing nothing but the reflection of oneself, in other words, a symbolic call for contemplation.[69]

IV

Sri Narayana Guru's scheme of social reform, as embodied in the S.N.D.P. Yogam, then, emerged as his most conspicuous legacy, for the reasons mentioned above, and because the existing injustices of Kerala society rendered such an organization of a discriminated outcaste community necessary for the attainment of their own rights. Izhavas' agitation for temple entry has already been noted. There were also other issues which warranted demonstration. Equal opportunity for education and employment in the government services with Brahmins and Nairs, who dominated the governments of Travancore and Cochin was one of them, in which case the non-Hindu population of these states, the Christians and the Muslims, also shared a grievance. The situation of the Izhavas in the province of Malabar, which was under direct British rule, was dramatically different, for reasons discussed above, which only helped to bring home more poignantly to their less fortunate brethren to the south the gravity of their problem.

68 *Rules of the S.N.D.P. Yogam*, Revised in 1966, (Ernakulam, 1966); *S.N.D.P. Union Rules* (Quilon, 1954); *Rules of S.N.D.P. Yogam Branches* (no date or place).
69 Nataraja Guru, interview; K. Balarama Panikar, interview; R. Sankar, interview.

The situation in Travancore was more explosive as, paradoxically enough, the relatively more enlightened kings of that state had introduced at least a semblance of representative government since 1888. The first representative body organized by King Sri Moolam in 1888 was to have five to eight members, all of whom were to be appointed by the king, and only two of them from outside the civil service. They had only an advisory role in the government. But as a result of subsequent reorganizations of this body, mainly provoked by popular agitation and pressure from the British Residents, the number of its members and its functions in the government increased. The 1932 reorganization was the most significant until then as it provided for two houses, an upper house with thirty-seven members, twenty-two of whom were to be elected, and a lower house with seventy-two members, of whom forty-three were to be elected. Although a few Izhavas served in the state's legislatures at various times, they were never fairly represented, nor was a fair representation of them possible under the 1932 regulations, as voting rights were restricted to property owners. For the right to vote in the election of the lower house one had to pay at least five Rupees in property taxes and twenty-five Rupees for the right to vote for the upper house. This provision, in effect, excluded the vast majority of Izhavas as well as most Muslims, Latin Christians,[70] and other outcaste Hindus. The following table indicates the relative paucity of eligible voters among these groups prior to the 1932 reorganization of the legislature.[71]

	1931 Population	1931 Eligible Voters
Total	5095973	145546
Total Hindus	3134888	96414
Nairs	868411	52936
Izhavas	869863	12163
Christians	1604475	40844
Muslims	353274	8288

Almost immediately after the royal proclamation reorganizing the legislature, the Izhavas raised their protest against the eligibility restrictions on voters and demanded assurance of a representation proportionate to their numbers. They were soon joined by Muslims and Christians to forge a powerful political coalition. As the joint appeal of these three communities was largely ignored by the government, they decided to boycott the election completely.

70 Latin Christians who follow the Roman rite are largely the descendants of the converts of St. Francis Xavier and other Western missionaries since the sixteenth century. As they came from mostly lower castes, many from Izhavas, their social condition is generally similar to that of low caste Hindus. The Syrian Christians or St. Thomas Christians, in contrast, claim to be the converts of St. Thomas the Apostle and descendants of high caste Hindu families. Whatever the validity of these claims, they historically enjoyed better social and economic conditions.

71 This table taken from Thazhava Kesavan, "Nivarthana Prakshobhanam," *S.N.D.P. Yogam Golden Jubilee Souvenir*, p. 227.

Although the king's government brought much pressure upon the leaders of these communities to participate in the election, the boycott turned out to be generally successful, as only twelve members of these communities weakened under pressure to allow themselves to be elected to the lower house and only three to the upper house. As their agitation continued, the scope of their demands also broadened to include other grievances, the most important of which was equal representation in government service.

The S.N.D.P. Yogam, and the Izhava community in general, was in the forefront of the agitations of the 1930's, which once again brought them face to face with the Brahmin-dominated caste system, of which they have been the principal victims in Kerala for many centuries. Their situation, being Hindus, was more intolerable than that of the Christians and Muslims who were spared much humiliation being outside the pale of Hinduism. The progress the Izhavas had made in the previous few decades under Sri Narayana Guru did not in any great measure mitigate their grievances, as the Guru's *advaita* (non-dualist, casteless) philosophy found no acceptance among caste Hindus, and his establishment of Izhava temples only helped to ghettoize them from the mainstream of Hindu life, thus in a way magnifying their distress. Thus they found themselves in a situation where they were totally disillusioned with Hinduism itself. It was understandable, then, why some of their leaders thought that the only way out of their misery was mass migration to non-Hindu religions. In fact, the S.N.D.P. Yogam formally resolved to do so in 1935.[72]

Large numbers of Izhavas had become Christians in various parts of Kerala over the previous centuries either under the influence of Catholic missionaries, the successors of St. Francis Xavier, or through the efforts of Protestant missionaries who had come in increasing numbers since the early part of the nineteenth century. Christianity had the added attraction of being the religion of the overlords of India, the English, which meant that a conversion to that religion promised special privileges and protection from the central government. Besides, the Christian missionaries not only welcomed but also actively promoted a movement in that direction. Therefore, a number of prominent Izhava leaders, most notably C. V. Kunjuraman, advocated mass conversion to Christianity. In fact, he proceeded to conduct negotiations with the Anglican bishop of Kottayam, Bishop Moor, for this purpose.[73]

Buddhism was another possibility. Izhavas' historic identification with Buddhist Ceylon, the distinct possibility of their Buddhist past, and the non-ritualistic and casteless character of the religion itself were strong reasons for adopting Buddhism. Several Izhava leaders, most importantly K. Ayyappan and C. Krishnan, advocated conversion to Buddhism. C. Krishnan even invited three Buddhist Bhikshus to Calicutt in 1935, built a *vihar* for them, and eventually became Buddhist himself along with some other prominent Izhava

---

72 Thazhava Kesavan, *ibid.*, p. 228.
73 M. C. Joseph, "Kshetrapravesanam," *Vivekodayam*, special issue, September 1968, pp. 104–105; K. Balarama Panikar, interview; K. Sukumaran, a private interview held at Trivandrum, August 1971.

friends,[74] a step which was expected to be followed by large numbers of Izhavas.

Other Izhavas looked to still other religions. For example, C. Kuttan and a few of his friends became Sikhs, and others thought Islam was the answer to their problems.[75]

However, such mass conversion efforts, although they were promoted by most prominent Izhava leaders, did not succeed for various reasons. For one thing, Sri Narayana Guru himself had put a damper on such efforts when conversion movements threatened a fragmentation of the Izhava community in the 1920's. To counter such movements he had convened a "conference of all religions" in Alwaye in 1921, where by proclaiming his famous principle: "Whatever be man's religion it is enough that he be good," he deemphasized the necessity of religious conversion.[76] But even more importantly, it was the timely action of the government of Travancore that abruptly put and end to the conversion efforts of the Izhavas. Threatened by the prospect of large numbers of Izhavas suddenly becoming Christians – Christianity was a greater threat than other religions because of the presence of eager missionaries under the protection of British overlords – thus creating dangerous imbalance in the population pattern of the state ruled by a Hindu king, the government suddenly decided to pay heed to the demands of the demonstrators. It was perhaps this threat more than the numerous petitions of the Izhava-Muslim-Christian coalition to the king, the British Vice Roy of India, the British Parliament, and the Central Legislature of India, and their demonstrations that brought about a resolution of their grievances in the royal proclamations of 1936 and 1937.[77] By far the most dramatic of these was the Temple Entry Proclamation of 1936 which opened all state owned temples to all Hindus, regardless of their caste, thus ending a discrimination that had lasted over a thousand years. Another proclamation of the same year opened "lower division" jobs to the whole population of the state, proportionate to their numbers, reserved forty percent of "intermediate division" jobs for the backward communities, and left the "upper division" jobs undetermined, but with the understanding that there would also be a *de facto* representation of all groups in them. The 1937 proclamation provided for fair representation of all groups in the legislature, reserving for the Izhavas eight seats in the lower house and two in the upper, and made similar provisions for the representation of Muslims, Latin Christians and other backward groups.[78]

---

74 M. C. Joseph, *ibid.*, Bhikshu Dharmaskandha (one of the original Bhikshus who arrived from Ceylon), letter to the author dated 8-10-1971, and in the introductory essays of *Mahabodhi Souvenir* (Calicut, 1964), pp. 1–2, 8, 26–28; C. V. Kunjuraman, *Budha Matha Pradeepam*, pp. 119–146; K. R. Achuthan, *C. Krishnan*, pp. 227–244.
75 M. C. Joseph, "Kshetrapravesanam," pp. 104–105; K. Balarama Panikar, interview; K. Sukumaran, interview.
76 Nataraja Guru, *Word of the Guru*, p. 388; K. Sukumaran and K. Balarama Panikar, interview.
77 M. C. Joseph, "Kshetrapravesanam," pp. 104–105; R. Sankar, K. Balarama Panikar, K. Sukumaran, interview.
78 For these I follow Thazhava Kesavan, "Nivarthana Prakshobhanam," pp. 225–230.

These favorable developments did not promise any dramatic changes in the condition of the Izhavas. Religiously and socially they were still outcastes, being required to obey humiliating caste regulations such as giving way to the Brahmins, without violating the prescribed thirty-six foot distance from them. The new rights they gained by the Temple Entry Proclamation were, then, more symbolic than real. The representation they received in the legislature and government service also did not bring about any great change in their condition, as these provisions did not increase in an appreciable measure their educational opportunities, nor did they result in a substantial change in their economic status because the economy of the state depended mostly on land holdings which were largely controlled by caste Hindus and some Syrian Christians.

It was only after Indian independence and as a result of the constitutional provisions for the advancement of backward classes that appreciable progress was made in the social and economic conditions of the Izhavas of Kerala as a whole, which is true of low castes everywhere in India. Article 15 of the Indian constitution included provisions for special privileges for backward classes, such as reserved seats in the central and state legislatures, guaranteed positions in government services, and special arrangement for admission and scholarships in schools, universities, and professional colleges – which privileges were distributed in varying degrees according to the needs of backward communities. Given the relatively better situation of the Izhavas, in comparison to the other low caste and backward communities of Kerala, and given their gains in political representation and government service, special provisions were made for them only in the area of education. Out of the thirty-five percent seats in the professional colleges set apart for backward communities, thirteen were reserved for them, and a substantial share of the ten percent seats earmarked for backward groups in arts and science colleges. The following table prepared by a state commission under Justice G. Kumara Pillai, which made a review of these special provisions for backward classes in Kerala in 1964, is indicative of the tremendous advantage they afforded to the Izhava community. The table deals with admission to pre-medical programs.[79]

Year	Total number of admissions	Number of admissions Izhavas would have received without reservation	Number of admissions Izhavas received because of reservation	% of actual admissions Izhavas would have received without reservation
1957–58	100	9	21	42.9
1958–59	100	6	18	33.3
1959–60	100	13	22	59.0
1960–61	100	8	19	42.0
1961–62	100	10	16	62.5
1962–63	100	7	15	46.7
1963–64	100	7	15	46.7

79 This table is taken from "'K.,' Kumara Pollai Commission Report: Oru Padhanam," *Vivekodayam*, Special Issue, January 1967, p. 197.

Izhavas also gained comparable advantages in other fields of education as well in the years since independence. For this and other reasons, the general condition of their community has appreciably improved, which was the reason that their special privileges were somewhat reduced in 1964, along with those of other backward communities,[80] as recommended by the Kumara Pillai commission which was in step with the spirit and provisions of the Indian constitution. Yet there is no doubt that the Izhavas have not achieved equality with the caste Hindus or Syrian Christians, religiously, socially, or economically.

Religiously and socially, caste Hindus still, by and large, continue to impose old caste regulations on Izhavas, in violation of the 1955 law abolishing the caste system. There have been at least 257 law suits in Kerala between 1956 and 1964,[81] stemming from such incidents, which certainly is only a very small fraction of similar cases that were never brought to public attention.

Economically, substantial strides have been made by the Izhava community, but a 1964 survey by the Kerala government Bureau of Economics and Statistics showed that they still lagged behind the major caste Hindu and Syrian Christian communities. For example, only 2.4% of the Izhavas owned five or more acres of land as opposed to 7.5% of Nairs, and only 3.8% of Izhava families had an income of 300 or more Rupees per month while the percentage of such Nair families was 8.8.[82]

The status of Izhavas in government service is still worse, perhaps because no special provisions were made for them since independence, as the 1967 situation indicates. The ratio of Izhavas in that year holding some of the high government jobs is as follows: I.A.S. and I.C.S. jobs (highest career administrative jobs) 64-1; district collectors 9-0; department heads 55-5; high court justices 12-2; government secretaries 10-1; district judges 20-3; I.P.S. jobs (lower level career administrative jobs) 28-3.[83] This indeed indicates a gross under-representation of a community that constitutes nearly thirty percent of the state's population.

Izhavas lagged behind in education, too, despite the many years of special privileges that they enjoyed. Here a possible explanation is the lack of proper motivation and stimulus, as the Izhava students come from relatively poor families and parents with little or no education, a situation comparable to the condition of the children in American ghettos. The 1964 statistics on school dropouts showed that out of all the Izhava children who entered the first grade only 13% reached the tenth grade as compared to 45% Brahmin, 33% Nair, and 32% Christian children which seems to substantiate the above theory.[84] Similar statistics on the percentage of Izhavas who completed elementary schooling, which in 1964 was 29% as opposed to the total state average of 47%

80   *Ibid.*, pp. 193–94.
81   *Ibid.*, p. 196.
82   *Ibid.*, p. 194.
83   *Ibid.*
84   Kumara Pillai Commission report, cited in *ibid.*, p. 196.

(which included the very backward classes as well), further confirms it.[85]

Some of the failures of the Izhavas in education seem to have resulted not so much from their own backwardness but from the historic prejudices against them that are still residued in society, and from their lack of financial resources to cope with a somewhat corrupt bureaucracy – which seems to be the only explanation for the following table about admission to the engineering colleges of Kerala, also prepared by the Kumara Pillai Commission in 1964.[86]

	Percentage of qualified applicants			Percentage of actual admissions			Percentage of the population
	1962–63	1963–64	1964–65	1962–63	1963–64	1964–65	
Izhavas	11.95	11.47	13.12	7.74	5.02	10.52	21.2*
Nairs	27.05	23.64	19.89	28.25	27.73	25.7	15.35
Christians	25.05	27.81	26.28	34.85	36.33	32.04	14.79

* This percentage figure is disputed; no separate census figures on Izhavas are available.

Considerable progress has been made by the Izhavas in all the areas mentioned above, since these statistics have been compiled. In the area of education they have made phenomenal advances, as the S.N.D.P. Yogam established in the 1960's more than a dozen institutions of higher education for the training of young Izhavas in liberal arts as well as in the professions, taking full advantage of the generous grants provided by the state and central governments for private education, not to mention their numerous new high schools and elementary schools. Their active participation in the notoriously tumultuous politics of the state also assured them increased representation in government jobs, and a fair share of the social and economic benefits accruing from various projects sponsored by the state and central governments.

In politics their preference has been the Communist Party, increasingly since the multi-party system became a reality in the state after a few years of complete control by the Congress Party in the wake of Indian independence. Statistics are not available, but without a doubt the majority of Izhavas support the Communist Party, either as cardholding members or by casting their votes, so much so that they are justly considered the mainstay of the Party. This phenomenon is variously explained as a sociological trend, an attraction for the economically promising political programs of the Communist Party;[87] as a classic class struggle where the working class Izhavas are pitted against the well-to-do caste Hindus and Syrian Christians;[88] as basically a defection from Hinduism because of the inequalities it imposes;[89] as a somewhat mis-

85   *Ibid.*
86   *Ibid.*, p. 197.
87   R. Sankar, interview.
88   P. S. Velayudhan, interview.
89   Murkot Kunhappa, interview.

guided attempt to return to a long lost tradition, that is the non-ritualistic and non-dogmatic, but scrupulously moral tradition of Buddhism;[90] and as a passing political fad with ideological overtones.[91] In any case, no one will doubt that this is a new phase in the continuing quest of the Izhavas for equality within the Kerala society.

---

90   K. Balarama Panikar, interview.
91   K. Sukumaran, interview.

Religion and the Secular: Categories for Religious Conflict and Religious Change in Independent India

ROBERT D. BAIRD

University of Iowa, Iowa City, U.S.A.

CONSTITUTIONAL PROVISIONS for "religion" in modern India and the subsequent determination of the realm of "religion" by the courts have been the study of several books by political scientists.[1] Legal scholars have also analyzed this material to determine the legal extent of religious freedom.[2] It is my intent to submit these documents to religio-historical analysis. Religio-historical analysis operates with the functional definition that religion is what concerns man ultimately. Religion is what is more important to him than anything else in the universe.[3] While religio-historical analysis can be used on materials which have traditionally been considered religious, it can also be useful in analyzing the religious dimensions of materials not commonly considered religious – in this case legal documents.

In these terms, *The Constitution of India* not only makes provision for "religion" in the modern Indian State, but is itself a religious document.[4] By providing a value structure for the modern Indian State, the Constitution not only orders priorities, but also embodies religious conflict and religious change.

1 Donald Eugene Smith, *India As a Secular State* (Princeton: Princeton University Press, 1963); Ved Prakash Luthera, *The Concept of the Secular State and India* (Calcutta: Oxford University Press, 1964).
2 N. A. Subramaniam, "Freedom of Religion," *Journal of the Indian Law Institute*, July–Sept., 1961, pp. 323–350; Harry E. Groves, "Religious Freedom," *Journal of the Indian Law Institute*, April–June, 1962, pp. 191–204; B. Parameswara Rao, "Matters of Religion," *Journal of the Indian Law Institute*, Oct.–Dec., 1963, pp. 509–513; J. Duncan M. Derrett, *Religion, Law and the State in India* (London: Faber and Faber, 1968); G. S. Sharma (ed.), *Secularism: Its Implications for Law and Life in India* (Bombay: N. M. Tripathi Private Ltd., 1966); V. K. Sinha (ed.), *Secularism in India* (Bombay: Lalvani Publishing House, 1968).
3 For a more extended treatment of this approach see the author's *Category Formation and the History of Religions* (The Hague: Mouton & Co., 1971).
4 For the purpose of this paper, "religion" will refer to the realm for which the Constitution provides freedom, while religion will refer to the functional definition of religion as ultimate concern.

The Constitution: The Conflict of Religions

When the study of religion is defined as the study of what people have considered of ultimate importance and the structure of reality consequent to such determinations, religion can take the form of a non-transcendent concern. The Constitutional religious model is non-transcendent. The Constitution neither affirms nor denies life beyond the present existence – it is simply not a relevant consideration. The preamble to the Constitution suggests the religious orientation of the document.

> WE, THE PEOPLE OF INDIA, having solemnly resolved to constitute India into a SOVEREIGN DEMOCRATIC REPUBLIC and to secure to all its citizens:
> JUSTICE, social, economic and political;
> LIBERTY of thought, expression, belief, faith and worship;
> EQUALITY of status and opportunity; and to promote among them all
> FRATERNITY assuring the dignity of the individual and the unity of the Nation;
> IN OUR CONSTITUENT ASSEMBLY this twenty-sixth day of November, 1949, do HEREBY ADOPT, ENACT AND GIVE TO OURSELVES THIS CONSTITUTION.

By limiting itself to concerns relating to this life, the Constitution stands in marked contrast with traditional religious models such as the one contained in the *Manusmṛti*.[5] For example, both the Constitution and *Manusmṛti* place considerable emphasis on justice. But in *Manusmṛti* the doctrines of karma and rebirth require that justice be defined in terms of considerations which take place before and after one's present existence. The Constitution defines justice in such a way that it must be actualized in the present existence. The doctrines of karma and rebirth are not denied – they are simply ignored.

Closely related to this is the fact that for the Constitutional religious model the content of justice is based on equality. All people are to be considered equal before the law and are to be afforded equal opportunity for employment, education and access to public facilities. Article 17 abolishes untouchability. If Article 16(4) provides for the possible reservation of positions for persons in backward classes, it is not because they are deemed superior, but because reverse discrimination seemed necessary to balance previously inherited handicaps which are themselves inconsistent with the theory of human equality.

By way of contrast, *Manusmṛti* rejects the inherent equality of all persons. Not limiting itself to this life, it interprets present inequalities as the result of past deeds. *Manusmṛti* begins with a chapter on creation in which the class system is seen as a part of the created order. Brahmans, Kṣatriyas, and Vaiśyas are to offer sacrifices and study the Vedas, and perform other functions peculiar to their respective classes. Śūdras are to serve the other classes. Since they are not *dvijas*, they do not have access to the Vedas nor do they perform sacrifices. Manu is declared to be omniscient and of equal authority with the Vedas.[6]

Because people are different by birth, justice must be dispensed so as to

---

5   G. Buhler (trans.), *The Laws of Manu*, Vol. XXV, S.B.E., (Delhi: Motilal Barnarsidass, reprint 1964). First published by Oxford University Press, 1886.
6   *Ibid.*, II, 7.

take such inequalities into account. Some men are lower than other men, and women are lower than men. *Manusmṛti* is as convinced that this is the way things are as the Constitution is that reality is not so structured. Women are by nature passionate and not to be trusted alone. They must be subject successively to their fathers, their husbands, and their sons.[7] Marriage should not be contracted with some kinds of people,[8] and contact with impure people renders one impure.[9] In implementing justice, *Manusmṛti* emphasizes the importance of honesty in testimony and trustworthiness in witnesses. Perjury has its penalty, but as in other cases the penalty is determined by where you stand in the class hierarchy.[10] And, if a Śūdra arrogantly goes against the nature of things by trying to teach Brahmans their duty, "the king shall cause hot oil to be poured into his mouth and into his ears."[11] Now this is conceived as a scheme of justice in that it indicates how one ought to conduct oneself in the light of the way things are. But assumed in this scheme are the notions of karma and rebirth. Life is not limited to the present and the mundane. Here lies a significant contrast between the Manu religious model and the Constitutional religious model.

The non-transcendent orientation of the Constitutional religious model is further revealed in the status given to more traditional religious expressions.[12] N. A. Subramanium has noted that "The importance of Articles 25 and 26 lies not so much in the *grant* of religious liberty but in its *restriction*."[13] Article 25 is subject to the other provisions of Part III of the Constitution regarding

---

7   *Ibid.*, V, 148.
8   *Ibid.*, III, 6–7.
9   *Ibid.*, V, 85.
10   *Ibid.*, VIII, 122–123.
11   *Ibid.*, VIII, 272.
12   Articles 25 and 26 of the Constitution read as follows:
      25. (1) Subject to public order, morality and health and to the other provisions of this Part, all persons are equally entitled to freedom of conscience and the right freely to profess, practise and propagate religion.
      (2) Nothing in this article shall affect the operation of any existing law or prevent the State from making any law –
            (a) regulating or restricting any economic, financial, political or other secular activity which may be associated with religious practice;
            (b) providing for social welfare and reform or the throwing open of Hindu religious institutions of a public character to all classes and sections of Hindus.
      Explanation I. – The wearing and carrying of *kirpans* shall be deemed to be included in the profession of Sikh religion.
      Explanation II. – In sub-clause (b) of clause (2), the reference to Hindus shall be construed as including a reference to persons professing the Sikh, Jaina or Buddhist religion, and the reference to Hindu religious institutions shall be construed accordingly.
      26. Subject to public order, morality and health, every religious denomination or any section thereof shall have the right –
            (a) to establish and maintain institutions for religious charitable purposes;
            (b) to manage its own affairs in matters of religion;
            (c) to own and acquire movable and immovable property; and
            (d) to administer such property in accordance with law.
13   *Loc. cit.*, p. 350.

"Fundamental Rights." These include the elimination of untouchability, equality before the law, and provisions for members of backward classes. Furthermore, religious freedom is "subject to public order, morality and health...," and cannot stand in the way of social reform.

Now these restrictions on the otherwise free exercise of "religion" constitute an admission that a conflict exists. It suggests that the Constitutional religious system may well be in conflict with traditional religious practices. Hence religious freedom cannot be granted without restriction. In the event that a conflict surfaces, the Constitution provides that the constitutional religious model will prevail. Traditional religious systems have the freedom to exist within the provisions of the Constitution. But those provisions make it clear that the traditional religious expressions cannot exist if they are in conflict with the Constitutional religious model. In cases where there is religious conflict of this nature, religious change becomes a necessity for survival. But the survival can be only partial, as the conflicting tradition is modified so as to ease the grounds for the conflict.

One of the devices for handling religious conflict is through the categories of "religion" and the "secular." According to the Constitutional religious model, life can be divided into these two all-encompassing categories. It is the category of "religion" which is granted freedom. But over against "religion" is the "secular" for which the same degree of freedom is not provided. Sometimes the realms of "religion" and the "secular" are closely related, but it is the view of the Constitution that they ought not to be confused.

"Religion" and the "secular" are not only part of the Constitutional religious model, but they are part of the religious conflict in that they run counter to much traditional religious thinking in India which sees life as homogeneous. In *Manusmṛti*, for example, the place of women, the nature of marriage, etc., are justified by the same sanction as more traditional "religious" matters. And, it has been common for Muslims to hold that personal law and inheritance was as much a matter of Muslim faith and tradition as was prayer. Such religious models did not consider "religion" as a segment of existence. Even the Supreme Court recognizes this to have been the case.

> ...Sometimes practices, religious and secular, are inextricably mixed up. This is more particularly so in regard to Hindu religion because as is well known, under the provisions of ancient Smritis, all human actions from birth to death and most of the individual actions from day to day are regarded as religious in character.[14]

These categories are not only a means for handling religious conflict and religious change, but are at the same time a part of the religious system whose survival is constitutionally guaranteed. Hence it is determined that the religious conflict will be handled through categories contained in one of the conflicting religions. These categories have become axiomatic, so that neither side of a litigation is able to deny the categories themselves. The categories are given sanction as part of the Constitutional religious model. Whether one is arguing

---

14 *Shri Govindlaji* v. *State of Rajasthan, All India Reporter.* 1963 SC 1638 at p. 1661.

his case on the side of the Constitutional religious model or from a more traditional point of view, the case must be made within these categories. Once the legitimacy of the two categories is no longer questioned, certain activities can be relegated to the "secular," thereby cut off from the Constitutional provisions for "religious" freedom. But when this method proves insufficient, other alternatives must be taken.

Although the categories of "religion" and the "secular" are an integral part of the Constitutional religious model, and although they are axiomatic, they are not constitutionally defined. This has been left to the courts. We now turn to the attempt at definition by the Supreme Court.

The Supreme Court: Defining "Religion" and the "Secular"

Supreme Court judgments reveal an ambivalence with reference to the definitional problem. The Court expresses a difficulty in distinguishing between the two realms when it says: "The question, is, where is the line to be drawn between what are matters of religion and what are not?"[15] In the case of a Mahant, for example, one is dealing with the spiritual leader of an institution who by virtue of his position also exercises wide powers of property management. Moreover, such a definition is not only difficult, it is virtually impossible. "The word 'religion' has not been defined in the Constitution and it is a term which is hardly susceptible of any rigid definition."[16] If the term "religion" is difficult to define, then "secular" would be no easier since its intelligent use presupposes a meaning for "religion."

While the Supreme Court states that there are difficulties in making the separation, the Constitution enjoins it, and there are times when the Court seems to make the required distinctions with little effort. There is no doubt, for example, that the administration of properties is a "secular" matter and thereby subject to law.

> It is clear, therefore, that questions merely relating to administration of properties belonging to a religious group or institution are not matters of religion to which clause (b) of the Article applies.[17]

In seeking to determine the limits of "religion," whose freedom from legislation is guaranteed, the definition offered by the American Supreme Court in *Davis* v. *Benson* (133 U.S. 333 at 342) is quickly discarded. That definition was:

> that the term "religion" has reference to one's views of his relation to his Creator and to the obligations they impose of reverence for His Being and character and of obedience to His will. It is often confounded with *cultus* of form or worship of a particular sect, but is distinguishable from the latter.[18]

15 *Commissioner, Hindu Religious Endowments, Madras* v. *Sirur Mutt, The Supreme Court Journal,* Vol. XXVI, 1954, p. 348.
16 *Ibid.*
17 *Ibid.*
18 *Ibid.*

Whatever view of "religion" the Supreme Court of India is to take it cannot define out of existence Buddhists and Jains (who do not affirm any Supreme Being).

"Religion" goes beyond mere belief. It can include ceremonies, ethical obligations and can even extend to matters of food and dress.

> A religion may not only lay down a code of ethical rules for its followers to accept, it might prescribe rituals and observances, ceremonies and modes of worship which are regarded as integral parts of religion, and these forms and observances might extend even to matters of food and dress.[19]

By taking account of the constitutional reference to the "practice of religion" (Article 25), the Supreme Court makes observable activity as much a part of "religion" as private belief systems. But since the State can legislate on matters which are economic, financial or political, the question still remains as to how far "religious practices" will be permitted to extend themselves. Communities might claim that almost anything is "religious" in order to be exempted from governmental control. How then has the Supreme Court attempted to distinguish "religion" from the "secular"?

In *Commissioner, Hindu Religious Endowments, Madras* v. *Sirur Mutt*, the Attorney-General from Madras State introduced the concept of essentiality as a means for determining what is to be granted freedom under Article 26(b). But since, in fact, the determination of essentiality already presupposed the identification of the realm of "religion," it did not advance the Court's ability to distinguish between "religion" and the "secular." The Attorney-General's argument was that "all secular activities, which may be associated with religion but which do not really constitute an essential part of it, are amenable to State regulation."[20] While rejecting implications which the Attorney-General wanted to draw from his observations, the Supreme Court nevertheless expressed itself on the subject on essentiality. "...What constitutes the essential part of a religion is primarily to be ascertained with reference to the doctrines of that religion itself."[21] Here, again, the determination of essentiality presupposes the identification of "the doctrines of that religion."

The manner in which essentiality presupposes the realm of "religion" and is therefore unable to define it is more clearly revealed in *Panachand Gandhi* v. *State of Bombay*.[22] In that case the manager of a Svetamber Jain public temple and the trustees of Parsi Panchayat Funds and Properties in Bombay challenged the validity of the Bombay Public Trusts Act of 1950. This Act required that the trustee of every religious or charitable trust register that trust. A fee of Rs. 25 was levied, and further fees were required to defray expenses incurred in regulating public trusts. Counsel for the appellants argued that

> ...according to the tenets of the Jain religion the property of the temple and its income exist for one purpose only, *viz.*, the religious purpose, and a direction to spend money

---

19 *Ibid.*, p. 349.
20 *Ibid.*
21 *Ibid.*
22 S.C.J., Vol. XVII, 1954, p. 480.

for purposes other than those which are considered sacred in the Jain scriptures would constitute interference with the freedom of religion.[23]

To spend religious funds for governmentally imposed fees would be contrary to Jain "religion." The judgment does not indicate how such an assertion was supported. Nevertheless, the Supreme Court rejected the contention as unsound.

These expenses are incidental to proper management and administration of the trust estate like payment of municipal rates and taxes, etc., and cannot amount to diversion of trust property for purposes other than those which are prescribed for any religion.[24]

Whether the objection of the appellants was sound or not, or whether it is in reality contrary to the Jain "religion" to pay such fees is less important for our analysis than the fact that here a religious institution through its counsel made a statement about the nature of its "religion" and it was not accepted by the Court. It is true that in order to gain one's ends before the Court such an argument may have been conjured up irrespective of the beliefs of the community. But it is the way the objection is handled that is instructive for our purposes. Although the religious institution made an explicit statement about their "religion," since it extended into the area which the Court considered the "secular" no further discussion was necessary.

In *Commissioner, Hindu Religious Endowments, Madras* v. *Sirur Mutt* it was stipulated that

a religious denomination or organization enjoys complete autonomy in the matter of deciding as to what rites and ceremonies are essential...[25]

It was also stipulated that just because such matters involved the outlay of funds they were not any less "religious." However, in *Panachand Gandhi* v. *State of Bombay* the power of the religious community to define the extent of its own "religion" does not extend beyond the sphere of "religion" as intended in the Constitution and explicated in the Courts. If it is determined that it is the "secular" role of government to register a trust to ensure its proper management, and if it is the constitutional right of the government to levy fees to defray the cost thereof, then this is part of the "secular" realm. Although the religious institution has unchallenged right to determine its own affairs in matters of "religion," the extent of that "religion" cannot reach into the constitutionally determined realm of the "secular." Hence, it can define its "religion" and what is essential to it, but only within the bounds of "religion" as distinct from the "secular." It becomes clear that the concept of essentiality is not helpful in defining "religion," since an assumed realm of "religion" is logically prior to essentiality. *Panachand Gandhi* v. *State of Bombay* does not resolve the question of how one determines what is "religion."

In *Shri Govindlalji* v. *State of Rajasthan*,[26] the applicability of the Nathdwara

---

23 *Ibid.*, p. 487.
24 *Ibid.*
25 *Loc. cit.*, p. 351.
26 A.I.R. 1963 SC 1638.

Temple Act of 1959 was challenged on the ground that the temple was the property of the Tilkayat and was not a public temple. The Court then attempted to determine if it was an essential part of the tenets of the Pushtimargiya Vaishnava Sampradaya that they could only worship in private temples owned and managed by the Tilkayat. They decided that it was not. But a new element arises.

The judgment of the Supreme Court reiterated that when one is deciding a religious practice it must be an essential or integral part of the "religion." And, this must be decided by whether the practice is considered integral by the community itself. But what if the community does not speak with a united voice?

> Take the case of a practice in relation to food or dress. If in a given proceeding, one section of the community claims that while performing certain rites white dress is an integral part of the religion itself, whereas another section contends that yellow dress and not the white dress is the essential part of the religion, how is the Court to decide the question.[27]

How will the Court decide? Gajendragadkar's judgment returns to essentiality. Unless this test is used, even secular practices might be confused with "religion."

> The question will always have to be decided by the Court and in doing so, the Court may have to inquire whether the practice in question is religious in character and if it is, whether it can be regarded as an integral and essential part of the religion, and the finding of the Court on such an issue will always depend upon the evidence adduced before it as to the conscience of the community and the tenets of its religion.[28]

A new problem is introduced: the possibility of lack of unanimity within a community. However, no new criterion is offered for determining the extent of "religion." But since in the above statement a practice's "religious" character comes prior to its essentiality, essentiality is again no help in determining "religiousness." And, no further indication is given as to the criterion that the Supreme Court will use to decide "if the practice in question is religious in character."

The difficulty which the Court has had in defining "religion" is not due to its indefinability. All communicable symbols are definable.[29] But the Court is unable to handle what has been considered "religion" within the categories of "religion" and the "secular," because to do so creates religious conflict and requires dealing with traditional religious expressions in terms provided by a new and conflicting religious model. The Supreme Court has been unsuccessful in defining the categories explicitly. But, defined or undefined, the categories continue to be used. How the Supreme Court handles the categories is a study of the progressive victory of the Constitutional religious model. That the victory is neither swift nor complete does not change the nature of the conflict nor the direction of the required religious change.

---

27   *Ibid.*, p. 1660.
28   *Ibid.*, pp. 1660–1661.
29   cf. *Category Formation and the History of Religions*, Chapter I.

The Supreme Court: When the Categories Are Adequate

Although "religion" and the "secular" are never clearly defined by the Court, they are nevertheless used to handle religious conflict. Sometimes a practice is declared unessential, while on other occasions the Court seems to act on its own advice in *Panachand Gandhi* v. *State of Bombay* that in difficult cases the "court should take a common-sense view and be actuated by considerations of practical necessity."[30]

In *Commissioner, Hindu Religious Endowments, Madras* v. *Sirur Mutt* it was held that the determination of what rituals were necessary was a "religious" matter, but that the scale of expenses for the rituals was a "secular" matter and could legitimately exist under governmental control. Financial matters, and the acquiring and administering of property are "secular" matters. Hence, there is no interference with "religion" if a governmentally appointed Commissioner oversees the daily affairs of the temple, for that is a "secular" matter.[31] When Sikhs contested governmental action legislating the method of representation on the Board which manages their Gurdwaras, it was determined that the manner of representation was "secular" and could be determined by the State.[32]

In *Bira Kishore Deb* v. *State of Orissa*,[33] it was argued that the Shri Jagannath Temple Act of 1954 deprived the Raja of Puri of his personal property. The appellant, in representing his case within the categories provided, distinguished two functions of the Raja. He was the chief servant of the temple (*adya sevak*) and also the sole superintendent in charge of the secular affairs of the temple. The Court accepted the categories and maintained that the Act in no way limited the Raja in his "religious" functions but only intended to regulate the "secular" affairs of the temple. Section 15, cl.(1) of the Act required that an appointed committee provide for the proper performance of worship in accord with the Record of Rights. The Court pointed out that there are two aspects to Sevapuja. The one aspect has to do with the provision of the proper materials for the puja and this is a "secular" matter. After this the servants use the materials according to the dictates of "religion." Section 15(1) of the Act deals with the "secular."

It seems clear that it is the committee that decides what is demanded by the Record of Rights and not the servant of the idol. And, it is the duty of the committee to see that the servants carry out the Record of Rights properly. Since this is intended as a guarantee of "religious" integrity, held the Court, it cannot be an interference with "religion." But what the *adya sevak* is left with is the performance of duties mandatory upon him as determined by the committee in the light of the Record of Rights.[34] Hence the determination of

---

30   S.C.J., Vol. XVII, 1954, p. 487.
31   *Digyadarshan R.R. Varu* v. *State of A.P.*, A.I.R. 1970 SC 181.
32   *Sardar Sarup Singh* v. *State of Punjab*, S.C.J., Vol. XXII, 1959, p. 1123.
33   A.I.R. 1964 SC 1501.
34   *Ibid.*, p. 1510.

duties which are "religious" in accord with the Record of Rights is not itself a "religious" determination. So long as the committee allows (even enforces) the sevaks to perform the duties, their "religious" rights have not been touched. The "secular" management of the temple includes not only the financial matters but also the determination of the "religious" rites demanded by the Record of Rights.

Several petitions representing Vaishnava and Saivite temples in Tamil Nadu contended that the Tamil Nadu Hindu Religious and Charitable Endowments (Amendment) Act (1970) infringed upon their "religious" rights in doing away with the hereditary right of succession to the office of Archaka (pujari) in their temples.[35] The petitioners held that their rights had been violated under Article 26(b) since

> The freedom of hereditary succession to the office of Archaka is abolished although succession to it is an essential and integral part of the faith of the Saivite and Vaishnavite worshippers.[36]

Examining the *Agamas*, the Court found that only a qualified Archaka could step inside the sanctum sanctorum. The touch of anyone else would defile the image. Moreover, a Saivite cannot serve in a Vaishnavite temple, nor can a Vaishnavite serve in a Saivite temple. It was this rule that the principle of hereditary succession was intended to protect. The Court agreed that failure to appoint a person from the appropriate denomination would "interfere with a religious practice the inevitable result of which would be to defile the image."[37]

In this regard the Court also expressed itself on the matter of essence. In effect, it rejected the contention that hereditary right was essential, but held that it was essential that the images not be polluted.

> An Archaka of a different denomination is supposed to defile the image by his touch and since it is of the essence of the religious faith of all worshippers that there should be no pollution or defilement of the image under any circumstances, the Archaka undoubtedly occupies an important place in temple worship. Any State action which permits the defilement or pollution of the image by the touch of an Archaka not authorized by the Agamas would violently interfere with the religious faith and practices of the Hindu worshipper in a vital respect, and would, therefore, be prima facie invalid under Article 25(1) of the Constitution.[38]

The Court admitted that the hereditary principle was common usage and was in practice from antiquity. "The real question, therefore, is whether such a usage should be regarded either as a secular usage or a religious usage."[39] It was the contention of the petitioners that it was indeed a "religious" practice. They held that priests who are to perform "religious" ceremonies may be

35 *Seshammal and Others* v. *State of Tamil Nadu, Supreme Court Cases.* Vol. II, Part I, 1972. pp. 11 ff.
36 *Ibid.*, p. 18.
37 *Ibid.*, p. 23.
38 *Ibid.*, pp. 20–21.
39 *Ibid.*, p. 24.

chosen by the temple on whatever basis the temple decides, and sometimes it is hereditary. They objected to the classification of the Act as social reform.

> Under the pretext of social reform, he (Mr. Palkhivala on behalf of the petitioners) contended, the State cannot reform a religion out of existence and if any denomination has accepted the hereditary principle for choosing its priest that would be a religious practice vital to the religious faith and cannot be changed on the ground that it leads to social reform.[40]

The Court agreed that the priest was appointed to a "religious" function, but questioned whether the appointment itself was "religious." Even the priest appointed in the hereditary manner is subject to the disciplinary power of the trustee. Furthermore, any lay founder of a temple can appoint a priest. Appointment is therefore by a "secular" authority, and hence it is a "secular" act. Neither the fact that some temples have followed the principle of heredity, nor the "religious" nature of what the Archaka does in the temple makes the act of appointment any less "secular."[41]

The Amendment Act was an expression of the Constitutional religious model.

> The Amendment Act was enacted as a step toward social reform on the recommendation of the Committee on untouchability, Economic and Educational development of the Scheduled Castes.[42]

As such, it posed a conflict with the traditional hereditary practices of denominational temples. The Court resolved the conflict in favor of the Act by declaring that, although what the Archaka did within the temple in his function as pujari was "religious," the appointment of the Archaka and the manner in which it was done was a "secular" matter, and legitimately under the jurisdiction of the State.

In *Saifuddin Saheb* v. *State of Bombay*,[43] the religious conflict which we are tracing is built into opposing judgments rendered by members of the Court, but resolved by the majority in terms of the categories of "religion" and the "secular." The issue at stake was whether the Bombay Prevention of Excommunication Act (1949) was in conflict with Articles 25 and 26 of the Constitution. The petitioner in the case was the Dai-ul-Mutlaq who was the head of the Dawoodi Bohra Community of Shia Muslims. Part of the Dai's authority was the power of excommunication. An earlier case determined that under certain conditions it was within the power of the Dai to excommunicate.[44] The petitioner argued that the practice of excommunication was essential, for without it the purity and continuity of the denomination could not be safeguarded by removing persons unsuitable for membership. It was further contended that the right to worship in a mosque and burial in a graveyard

---

40 *Ibid.*
41 *Ibid.*, p. 25.
42 *Ibid.*, p. 12.
43 A.I.R. 1962 SC 853.
44 A.I.R. 1948 PC 66.

dedicated to the community were "religious" rights not to be enjoyed by persons rightly excommunicated.

It was the contention of the State of Bombay that the Dai had the right to regulate religious practices but that excommunication was not an essential part of the "religion" of the Dawoodi Bohra community and hence was a "secular" matter which affected the civil rights of persons.

The religious conflict which we have been tracing becomes explicit in a contention of the Attorney-General for the State of Bombay when he argued that in abolishing excommunication the Act was "in consonance with modern notions of human dignity and individual liberty of action even in matters of religious opinion and faith and practice."[45] The preamble to the Act itself includes the following words: "And whereas in keeping with the spirit of changing times and in the public interest it is expedient to stop the practice..."

In his minority judgment, Sinha, C.J., interprets the Act as the culmination of the history of social reform which began with provisions of the Bengal Code which were later incorporated in the Caste Disabilities Removal Act of 1850. Again, the conflict with a new religious system arises:

> The impugned Act, thus, has given full effect to modern notions of individual freedom to choose one's way of life and to do away with those undue and outmoded interferences with liberty of conscience, faith & belief. It is also aimed at ensuring human dignity and removing all those restrictions which prevent a person from living his own life so long as he did not interfere with similar rights of others. The legislature had to take the logical final step of creating a new offence by laying down that nobody had the right to deprive others of their civil rights simply because the latter did not conform to a particular pattern of conduct.[46]

In coming to his decision, Sinha, C.J., introduced a slightly different category. Instead of merely speaking of "religion" and the "secular," he referred to excommunication as not being "purely religious" or "wholly religious." It has been recognized that the separation of "religion" from the "secular" was not simple. But when an act is not "purely religious" this means that there are civil consequences to the activity under consideration.[47] As a member of the Court, Sinha, C.J., held that he was not called upon to comment upon the "purely religious aspects" of excommunication, nor was he interested in distinguishing what they might be. He was responsible for making a judgment about actions touching on the civil rights of members of the community. Since excommunication treated the excommunicated much as a pariah, and since the Constitution abolished untouchability, the Act is valid. Sinha, C.J., then, decided in favor of the civil rights while recognizing implications for "religion" which did not concern him.

> Hence, although the Act may have its repercussions on the religious aspect of excommunication, in so far as it protects the civil rights of the members of the community, it has not gone beyond the provisions of Art. 25(2)(b) of the Constitution.[48]

---

45   A.I.R. 1962 SC pp. 859–860.
46   *Ibid.*, pp. 860–861.
47   *Ibid.*, p. 865.
48   *Ibid.*

The majority of the Court judged the Act unconstitutional. In arguing for the essentiality of excommunication, Das Gupta, J., appealed to an article in *Encyclopedia of Social Sciences* on "Excommunication" where it was argued that the practice had been a principal means of maintaining discipline and solidarity in a religious community. Furthermore, it was noted that at the time of initiation the Dawoodi Bohras take an oath of unquestioning faith and loyalty to the Dai. Das Gupta, J., indicated that this did not demand an answer to the question of whether every case of excommunication by the Dai was based on "religious" grounds. But by invalidating excommunication on any ground, the Act made it impossible to maintain the strength and continuity of the "religion."

> What appears to be clear is that where an excommunication is itself based on religious grounds such as lapse from the orthodox religious creed or doctrine (similar to what is considered heresy, apostasy or schism under the Canon Law) or breach of some practice considered as an essential part of the religion by the Dawoodi Bohras in general, excommunication cannot but be held to be for the purpose of maintaining the strength of the religion.[49]

What does Das Gupta, J., do with the attendant "civil rights" which are thereby curtailed? He does exactly what Sinha, C.J. did with the "religious" matters entailed in his "civil decision." They are secondary and are not his concern.

> The fact that civil rights of a person is affected by the exercise of this fundamental right under Art. 26(b) is therefore of no consequence.[50]

In this case the majority argument was in favor of the traditional practice. But it is interesting to note that although both sides of the Court made their decisions as though the categories were adequate to handle the conflict, both had to ignore one side of it. Both seemed to recognize that excommunication had a "religious" and a "secular" or civil side. Sinha, C.J. acted in the light of the "secular," ignoring the "religious," while the majority judgment passed on "religion" ignoring the "secular." So the conflict is resolved by the power of the Court, but not because the categories of "religion" and the "secular" adequately handled it. We will now turn to instances where the breakdown is even more apparent.

The Supreme Court: When the Categories Are Inadequate

In some instances additional methods or principles have been introduced to assist "religion" and the "secular." Three of these are reification, superstition, and the rule of harmonious construction.

Reification

Reification is the treatment of an historical process characterized by diversity and change as a single objective entity. In the study of religion it is

---

49 *Ibid.*, p. 869.
50 *Ibid.*

the treatment of "Hinduism," "Buddhism," and the like, as units of thought and practice.[51] Where there exists a conflict between the religious claims of a community and the Constitutional religious model, the Court has used reification in aid of "religion" and the "secular."

This method is particularly useful in reinforcing the Constitutional model in *M. H. Quareshi* v. *State of Bihar*.[52] Contesting the constitutionality of three acts for the prevention of cow slaughter, the petitioners argued that their fundamental rights guaranteed under Article 25 of the Constitution were abridged, since it was their custom to sacrifice a cow on Bakr Id Day. The petitioners claimed that this was enjoined in the Holy Quran, but the Court contended that the verses referred to merely stipulated that people should pray and offer sacrifice. Operating under a reified concept of Islam, the Court made a search for a scriptural statement making the sacrifice of a cow obligatory. A lack of obligatoriness would suggest that the practice was not essential to Muslim faith. Although the petitioners pointed out that it was their custom to sacrifice a cow, and although this was not denied by the Court, their custom was not sufficient. By treating Islam as a reified entity and considering the petitioners as Muslims, their specific contemporary practices could be ignored. When it was found that it was optional for a Muslim (according to "Hamilton's translation of Hedaya Book XLIII at page 592") to sacrifice a cow or camel for every seven persons or a goat for each person, it was apparent that for Muslims there was an option. Since the petitioners were Muslims, it must be optional for them as well. Although financial considerations would put the option out of reach for many, that was considered an economic matter and not a "religious" one. Since the sacrifice of a cow was optional for Muslims, it was optional for these Muslims, and since it was optional it was not essential, and since it was not essential it was not protected under Article 26 of the Constitution.

> We have, however, no material on record before us which will enable us to say, in the face of the foregoing facts, that the sacrifice of a cow on that day is an obligatory overt act for a Mussalman to exhibit his religious belief and idea.[53]

Superstition

Another concept which presents possibilities for use beyond its present actualization is the principle of superstition. In *Durgah Committee* v. *Hussain Ali*,[54] the issue was the respective rights of attendants of the shrine of Nasrat Khawaja Moin-ud-din Chishti in Ajmer. The shrine was run by the Chishti order of Sufis and the issue was the result of the Durgah Khawaja Saheb Act of 1955. In the judgment, written by Justice Gajendragadkar, the previous decisions relating to Articles 25 and 26 were recounted. But he also thought it advisable to "strike a note of caution." Once it was stated that practices were as much a part of "religion" as beliefs, it became possible for all kinds of

---

51   cf. *Category Formation and the History of Religions*, Chapter V.
52   S.C.J., Vol. XXI, 1958, p. 975.
53   *Ibid.*, p. 985.

practices to be judged "religious" by a given community. It was possible that even with the criterion of essentiality there might be practices which conflicted with the Constitutional religious model. Such practices would appear to fit under the Court's interpretation of Article 26, but they still could not be accorded the freedom stipulated therein. There is a difference between essential "religion" and superstitious accretions which may attach themselves to that csscncc in history.[55] Hence an historical community might sincerely believe that a practice is essential to their "religion," but that is because they mistake superstition for "religion."

> Similarly even practices though religious may have sprung from merely superstitious beliefs and may in that sense be extraneous and unessential accretions to religion itself.[56]

No definition of superstition is offered and the principle does not play a role in deciding this case.

In *Yagnapurushdasji* v. *Muldas*,[57] the issue was whether the temples of the Swaminarayan Sampradaya sect come under the Bombay Hindu Places of Public Worship Act (1956), since the appellants contended that they were not Hindus but a separate religion. At the end of a lengthy consideration of the nature of Hinduism and the tenets of the Swaminarayan Sampradaya sect it was concluded that they were Hindus. Of some importance was the fact that the sect had not objected to being so classified in Census reports. This case was decided as a matter of social reform. But Gajendragadkar J., held that although the contention of the sect began in sincerity, it was founded on superstition.

> It may be conceded that the genesis of the suit is the genuine apprehension entertained by the appellants; but as often happens in these matters, the said apprehension is founded on superstitition, ignorance and complete misunderstanding of the true teaching of Hindu religion and of the real significance of the tenets and philosophy taught by Swaminarayan himself.[58]

The use of this concept is seen to go hand in hand with reification. First, there was a determination of the essential tenets of Hinduism. Since the appellants contended that they were not Hindus, it was also necessary to find out what the Swaminarayan sect ought to believe if it were true to its founder. The result of the Court's research was that, although the appellants were sincere in their contention, they did not properly understand their own faith. And, not to understand one's own faith is to operate with "superstition, ignorance, and complete misunderstanding..."

---

54 A.I.R. 1961 SC 1402.
55 For a discussion of Gajendragadkar's view of the essence of "religion" see the author's "Mr. Justice Gajendragadkar and the Religion of the Indian Secular State," *Journal of Constitutional and Parliamentary Studies*, Oct.–Dec., 1972, Vol. VI, No. 4, pp. 47–64.
56 A.I.R. 1961 SC p. 1415.
57 A.I.R. 1966 SC 1119.
58 *Ibid.*, p. 1135.

The Rule of Harmonious Construction

In *Sri Venkataramana Devaru* v. *State of Mysore*,[59] the Gowda Saraswath Brahman sect contended that the Madras Temple Entry Authorization Act (1947) which opened their temple dedicated to Sri Venkataramana to all Hindus was in violation of Article 26(b) of the Constitution. They held that who was entitled to participate in temple worship was a matter of "religion." Admitting the precedent that "religion" includes practices as well as beliefs, the Court proceeded to determine whether exclusion of a person from a temple was a matter of "religion" according to "Hindu ceremonial law."[60] The Court observed that along with the growth of temple worship, there also grew up a body of literature called *Agamas* which stipulated how the temple was to be constructed, where the principal deity was to be consecrated, and where the other deities are to be installed. One such text includes degrees of participation.

> In the Nirvachanapaddathi it is said that Sivadwijas should worship in the Garbhagri-ham, Brahmins from the ante chamber or Sabah Mantabham, Kshatriyas, Vyasias (sic) and Sudras from the Mahamantabham, the dancer and the musician from the Nritha-mantabham east of the Mahamantabham, and that castes yet lower in scale should content themselves with the sight of the Gopurum.[61]

It is pointed out by the Court that violation of such regulations results in pollution of the shrine and requires purificatory ceremonies. In a 1908 case, *Sankarakinga Nadam* v. *Raja Rajeswara Dorai*,[62] it was agreed by the Privy Council that trustees who agreed to admit persons into the temple whom the Agamas did not permit were guilty of breach of trust. The Court agreed that temple entry was a matter of "religion."

> Thus under the ceremonial law pertaining to temples, who are entitled to enter into them for worship and where they are entitled to stand and worship and how the worship is to be conducted are all matters of religion.[63]

But another factor had to be taken into account. Article 25(2)(b) of the Constitution provides that nothing in the Article should prevent the State from making a law

> providing for social welfare and reform or the throwing open of Hindu religious insti-tutions of a public character to all classes and sections of Hindus.

The Court admitted that "the two Articles appear to be apparently in con-flict."[64] The position of the "Hindu social reformers" which culminated in Article 17 of the Constitution abolishing untouchability was then recounted. The reformers objected that "purely on grounds of birth" some Indians were denied access to public roads and institutions which were open to the general

---

59 S.C.J., Vol. XXI, 1958, p. 382.
60 *Ibid.*, p. 389.
61 *Ibid.*, p. 390.
62 I.L.R. 31 Mad.
63 S.C.J., Vol. XXI, 1958, p. 390.
64 *Ibid.*, p. 391.

Hindu public. This was not defensible on "any sound democratic principle."

After considerable argumentation it was finally admitted that this case involved two constitutional provisions, Article 26(b) and Article 25(2)(b), which are of equal authority. Appeal was then made to the "rule of harmonious construction" whereby two conflicting provisions are interpreted in such a manner as to give effect to both. The Court then agreed to the opening of the temple to all classes of Hindus. The right of the denomination to exclude members of the public from worshipping in the temple, although protected under Article 26(b), must give way to Article 25(2)(b). But this does not mean that anyone can go into any part of the temple at any time. Hence the denomination was permitted the right to exclude the general public from certain religious services. The Court felt that it had given effect to both provisions inasmuch as even after the exclusion from certain religious services, "what is left to the public of the right of worship is something substantial and not merely the husk of it."[65]

In this case the Court faced the existence of religious conflict. On the surface the solution seems sensible. But in terms of religio-historical analysis it must be observed that while a portion of the denominational right under Article 26(b) was preserved, another portion was taken away. For, while traditional religious practice as described in the *Agamas* did distinguish degrees of participation and involvement in temple worship, it also included the degree of exclusion. Some persons were to "content themselves with the sight of the Gopurum." The issue of temple pollution was ignored by the Court. The judgment said, in effect, that traditional practices could not be maintained in their entirety because Article 25(2)(b) denied such practices. Part of the denomination's traditional religious practices are maintained under the "rule of harmonious construction." But under the same principle another rather significant portion of their religion must be eliminated. This case, then, admits the existence of religious conflict and again implements religious change. It may also point out the inadequacy of the categories of "religion" and the "secular" to solve the issues of religious conflict introduced by the Constitutional religious model.

A religio-historical analysis of *The Constitution of India* and later Supreme Court cases reveals the existence of religious conflict. The categories of "religion" and the "secular" both provoke and also attempt to resolve the conflict. Although these categories have not been defined, and although they frequently prove inadequate, they nevertheless continue to be used. They are one means whereby the Supreme Court has attempted to resolve the conflict in favor of the Constitutional religious model.

---

65   *Ibid.*, p. 396.

Dilemmas of Secularism in Bangladesh

JOSEPH T. O'CONNELL

University of Toronto, Canada

THE PEOPLE's Republic of Bangladesh, now in its fourth year since liberation (December 16, 1971), still faces a formidable array of problems. One of these which is fundamental concerns the need to forge an effective sense of national identity and national purpose. To an extent, this sense of identity and purpose exists already, but it is doubtful that its present form and degree of intensity will prove sufficient to maintain cohesion and stimulate developmental change. I am viewing this problem as a religious one, meaning by this "one's way of valuing most intensively and comprehensively."[1] Commitment to the cause of defending or consolidating a new nation, if made wholeheartedly, is bound to involve what a person values intensively and in a comprehensive manner. If one happens to be a faithful Muslim, Hindu, Christian or Buddhist (as most citizens of Bangladesh claim to be), then his traditional religious faith must impinge in some way upon his patriotic or civic commitment. In a similar way, the humanistic religious values of an agnostic or atheistic individual influence his civic commitments. If serious conflicts develop at the level of intensive and comprehensive valuing between a person's theological or humanistic commitments and his civic commitments, then he will be confused and hampered in his activity. If vast numbers of persons experience a similar predicament at the level of religious valuing, then the morale of a nation can be undermined. By discussing the dilemmas of secularism in Bangladesh I wish to examine a problem of this sort as it affects the Muslims of Bangladesh, who number upwards of sixty million and who account for about eighty-five per cent of the nation's population.

These remarks are intended as introductory only, and in places are speculative. My training is not in the analysis of religion and politics but in the religious history of Bengali-speaking people, for which reason I spent eleven months (September 1972–July 1973) in Bangladesh reading materials for a historical anthology of Bengali Muslim writings. The remarks herein are based upon observations and conversations during that period, combined with reflection and further conversations with Bengalis upon returning to Canada, all against the background of reading in Bengali religious history. I offer apologies

---

1 Frederick Ferré, "The Definition of Religion," *Journal of the American Academy of Religion*, 38 (1970), 3–16.

in advance for failing to understand many things and for any unintended lapses from tact or discretion.

I. Secularism: The Fourth Principle of State Policy

The official pattern of national identity and purpose of Bangladesh is given in the Constitution passed by the Constituent Assembly on November 4, 1972:

> Pledging that the high ideals of nationalism, socialism, democracy and secularism, which inspired our heroic people to dedicate themselves to, and our brave martyrs to sacrifice their lives in, the national liberation struggle, shall be the fundamental principles of the Constitution;...[2]

Promulgation of this Constitution in less than a year after liberation was a remarkable achievement which I do not mean to belittle when I point to the dilemmas and difficulties that cluster around the fourth of the "high ideals," more popularly called "pillars" of state policy, namely, secularism. To begin with, the word "secularism" is ambiguous enough in English, suggesting ideological commitment in some contexts, neutral processes such as urbanization in other contexts. It is in fact a symbol of progress to some persons and of blasphemy to others. Even the related word "secularization" in Donald E. Smith's technical analysis has four different aspects which usually do not appear all together in a given historical case.[3] "Secularism" in the Bangladesh Constitution is offered as the equivalent of the Bengali word *dharma-nirapekṣatā*, which one would expect to see translated as "neutrality in religion," or simply "tolerance." Were it certain that the Bengali term and the history behind it are to dominate legal and judicial interpretation of the fourth pillar, then some of the ambiguity and strain engendered by the word "secularism" would evaporate. The English version of the Constitution is designated as the "Authorized English Translation," thus suggesting that the Bengali text is *the* Constitution. However, the document was composed first in English by lawyers trained in the British legal tradition as adapted to India and Pakistan, so "secularism" may be the concept intended by the founders after all. To indicate the variance between the English and the Bengali versions I shall write "secularism/tolerance" whenever referring to the fourth pillar. A further elaboration of secularism/tolerance is given in the Constitution's explanations of the four principles of state policy.

> 9. The unity and solidarity of the Bangalee nation, which, deriving its identity from its language and culture, attained sovereign and independent Bangladesh through a united and determined struggle in the war of independence, shall be the basis of Bangalee nationalism.
> 10. A socialist economic system shall be established with a view to ensuring the attainment of a just and egalitarian society, free from the exploitation of man by man.

---

2 Preamble to *The Constitution of the People's Republic of Bangladesh* (Authorized English Translation), passed by the Constituent Assembly of Bangladesh on November 4, 1972, and authenticated by the Speaker on December 14, 1972.
3 Donald Eugene Smith, *Religion and Political Development* (Boston: Little, Brown and Company, 1970), pp. 85–86.

11. The Republic shall be a democracy in which fundamental human rights and free-
    doms and respect for the dignity and worth of the human person shall be guaranteed,
    and in which effective participation by the people through their elected representa-
    tives in administration at all levels shall be assured.
12. The principle of secularism shall be realized by the elimination of –
    (a) communalism in all its forms;
    (b) the granting of the State of political status in favour of any religion;
    (c) the abuse of religion for political purposes;
    (d) any discrimination against, or persecution of, persons practising a particular
        religion.

The Constitution does not define secularism/tolerance directly. Rather, it
lists the abuses, the elimination of which will realize secularism/tolerance. The
first abuse, communalism, goes undefined altogether. Presumably it intends
such elements as: placing religious communal interests above the national
interest; subordinating civil rights to the whims of the dominant community;
obscuring political and economic exploitation by appeals to religious ideals;
and spreading a mood of communal intolerance and religious bigotry, so that
in times of tension members of the minority community are subject to harassment. It is clearly a pejorative term, reflecting the bad experience of communal
politics associated with the Pakistani period.

Another article of the Constitution enlarges upon the prohibition of "the
abuse of religion for political purposes." It states:

38. Every citizen shall have the right to form associations or unions, subject to any
    reasonable restrictions imposed by law in the interests of morality or public order:
        Provided that no person shall have the right to form, or be a member of, any
    communal or other association or union which in the name of or on the basis of any
    religion has for its object, or pursues, a political purpose.

This provision has major political implications because it seems to outlaw
any such parties as the Muslim League, the Jamā 'at-i Islāmi, as well as any
Hindu, Christian, or Buddhist political party. Does it prohibit lobbying or
public opinion formation on political matters by communal groups as well?
The provision is a much more rigorous curtailment of religious communal
activity than, for instance, anything in the Indian Constitution. In view of the
tendency of Muslims to view political and social affairs as religiously significant, as areas in which the divine injunction to establish a good and just
society is operative, the prohibition of all religio-political activity, if that is
how the Constitution is to be interpreted, is a bold move. Are the Muslims of
Bangladesh ready to abide by such a restriction? Perhaps they are in view of
the bad experience with communal politics in Pakistan, but it is also possible
that the Constitution, accepted less than a year after liberation in a Constituent
Assembly with virtually no opposition, may have gone beyond what the
typical Bengali Muslim will eventually find acceptable. Examples of radical
secularism are to be found within the Muslim world, notably in Turkey, but
in such cases a dominant modernizing elite has *imposed* changes, not, as in
Bangladesh, making popular democracy a fundamental principle of state
policy. While it is hazardous to guess what specific issues may prove con-

troversial, any application of the principle of secularism/tolerance that is viewed by the typical Muslims of Bangladesh as offensive to Islam will meet with widespread resistance.

The First Five-Year Plan, 1973–78, into which has gone at least as much thought as into the Constitution, has this to say about secularism/tolerance:

> 1.3. Secularism
>
> True to our secular belief, we stand committed to disband all communal forces from the body politic. The War of Liberation against the colonial oppressors which we waged as one man demonstrated that Bangladesh is able to rise above religious bigotry and differences of caste and creed. Even though decades of obscurantism and religious fanaticism cannot be obliterated in one day, such bigotry will not be able to thrive on the soil of Bangladesh if communalism ceases to be a political weapon. Our struggle for emancipation has highlighted our homogeneity and our struggle against poverty will only strengthen it.
>
> 1.4. Socialism
>
> However the ideal of socialism cannot be translated into reality as easily or as quickly as the other three principles of State policy. In Bangladesh today it remains a vision and a dream...[4]

This statement of the Planning Commission is noteworthy for its religious tone ("True to our secular belief, we stand committed...") and its dynamic resolve "to disband all communal forces..." There is more here than separation of religion and politics, more than guarantees of civil rights. There is a pledge not only to exclude communal forces from politics but to disband them. Paragraph 1.4. suggests this can be done relatively "easily and quickly," while paragraph 1.3. concedes that it cannot be done in a day. The decisive issue is bound up with the "if": "if communalism ceases to be a political weapon," bigotry will cease to thrive. There is no discussion of how this can be accomplished. Presumably, the Constitutional prohibition of mixing religion and politics is the fulcrum for effecting this desideratum.

A third source of guidance on the meaning of secularism/tolerance is the Prime Minister, Bangabandhu Sheikh Mujibur Rahman. Since he insists that the Constitution of 1972 is a faithful implementation of the proposals contained in the Manifesto of the Awami League prepared for the election of 1970, we may first consider what the Manifesto says about Islam and the minorities.

> Islam. The favored religion of the vast majority of the population is Islam. On this matter the Awami League has decided that there will be in the Constitution very clear guarantees that no law will be formulated or enforced in Pakistan contrary to the laws of Islam well established in the Holy Qur'ān and the Sunnah. There will be guarantees firmly established in the Constitution for preserving the purity of the numerous religious institutions. Adequate arrangements will be made for extending religious instruction at all levels.
>
> Minority. The minorities will enjoy full equal rights in the eyes of the law and will receive equal protection of the law. They will enjoy rights as citizens. The rights of the

---

4 Planning Commission, Government of the People's Republic of Bangladesh, *The First Five-Year Plan, 1973–1978* (Dacca, 1973), part I, chap. I, pars. 1.3–1.4.

minorities in the matter of preserving and preaching their own religion, in establishing and operating religious institutions, and in giving religious instructions to the adherents of their respective religions will be protected by the Constitution. No individual of a minority community will be required to pay taxes for the preaching of any religion but his own. No individual will be forced to accept any religious regulations nor be required to participate in any religious worship or program not connected with his own religion.[5]

The Constitution of Bangladesh seems to assure the various rights and protections promised minorities, and on the same ground the majority. However, there is no explicit guarantee within the Constitution that excludes legislation contrary to the law of Islam as established in the Qur'ān and the Sunnah, although the pledge to do so is expressly given by the Sheikh in at least one of his pre-election speeches.[6] Presumably it would be argued that in view of the democratic character of the Constitution the large majority of Muslims have adequate assurance that un-Islamic laws will not be enacted. In the incomplete collection of the Sheikh's pre-election speeches to which I have access explicit references to the Qur'ān and Sunnah are rare. The Sheikh is more apt to observe that in a country with eighty-five per cent of its population Muslim it is silly or an evidence of poor faith to suppose that anything repugnant to the teachings of Islam could be enacted. What he would consider repugnant to Islam, however, he does not elaborate beyond very general ethical ideals. For example,

> The slanderous rumor is being circulated against us that we are not believers in Islam. In reply to this assertion our statement is very clear. We are not believers in the Islam that is simply a label. We believe in the Islam of justice. Our Islam is the Islam of the holy and merciful prophet, which Islam has taught the inhabitants of the world the unfailing teaching of right and justice.[7]

On the whole, the pre-election speeches of Sheikh Mujibur Rahman contain relatively few references to Islam. There are a number of brief appeals to God and there is the occasional, somewhat exasperated, assertion that he and his followers are at least as good Muslims as those hypocrites who slander them. The guarantees to Muslims and to minorities occur occasionally, though the expression *dharma-nirapekṣatā* (religious neutrality, tolerance) does not seem to appear, nor the word "secularism," though some other English words creep in. The speeches, for the most part, are on the level of mundane political and economic interests.[8]

---

5   "Manifesto of the Awami League," in Sheikh Mujibur Rahman, *Mujibarera racanā samgraha* (Calcutta: Reflect Publications, 1378, i.e., 1971), p. 120. Hereafter cited as *Racanā*. English renderings of selections from this volume are mine.

6   Speech of October 10, 1970, in *Racanā*, p. 55.

7   Speech with no date in *Racanā*, p. 65.

8   *Racanā*, pp. 1 (vs. charge of conspiring against Islam); 2 (enemies deceive people in name of Islam); 54 (opposes communalism, pledges to protect minorities); 55 (vs. charge of undermining Islam); 61 (exploiters appeal to Islam); 64 (Muslims, Hindus, Christians, Buddhists are all Bengalis); 66 (no discrimination for religion or caste); 68 (majority and minority are all Bengalis); 76 (vs. the self-proclaimed lords of Islam); 79 (no more molestation of Hindus, Christians, Buddhists); 89 (every resident of Bangladesh is a Bengali and will be protected); 96 (all Bengalis – Muslim, Hindu, Christian, Buddhist –

It is after independence that, as Prime Minister, Sheikh Mujibur Rahman makes reference to the four pillars of the state and it would seem from the sampling of his speeches I have seen that only then does he speak more fully, though still not a great deal, about religion and communalism. On the seventh of June, 1972, he says:

> Secularism does not mean the absence of religion. You are a Mussalman, you perform your religious rites. The Hindus, the Christians, the Buddhists all will freely perform their religious rites. There is no irreligiousness on the soil of Bangladesh but there is secularism. This sentence has a meaning and that meaning is that none would be allowed to exploit the people in the name of religion, or to create such fascist organizations as the Al-Badr, Razakars, etc. No communal politics will be allowed in the country. Have you understood my four pillars?[9]

Another speech in which the Prime Minister makes extended reference to religion and secularism is one delivered to the Awami League in January, 1974.[10] In it he remarks that "the people of my Bangladesh are religious and God-fearing. They can be misled more easily in the name of religion than by any other means." It is likely that this insight, based upon bitter experience, underlies the Prime Minister's espousal of secularism/tolerance, rather than any ideological rationale. One can almost visualize the firm hand of the Father of the Country laying down the law to his pious but overly credulous children: "No more of this nonsense. It is dangerous. Do you understand?" So long as the father's prestige is sacrosanct, there is not apt to be serious objection, but one wonders if absolute severance of religious concerns from the political sphere will prove an effective long-term mechanism for ending the exploitation of religion for political purposes, especially when a by-product of the Constitutional restriction is a general inhibition against discussing in public any constructive relationships between Muslim solidarity and ideals and the national identity and purpose. The same speech is noteworthy also for its warning that communalism is on the rise again in rural Bangladesh.

> One who loves man can never be a communalist. Those of you who are Muslims must remember that Allah is Rabbul Alamin (Lord of all Mankind) and not Rabbul Muslimin (Lord of all the Mussalmans). All men are equal in His eyes, be he a Hindu, a Christian, a Muslim, a Buddhist. That is why those who spread the virus of communalism while talking of socialism and progress are wrong. Socialism and progress cannot co-exist with communalism. They are poles apart. Beware of those who want to sow the seeds of communalism in the soil of Bangladesh. You workers of the Awami League, you have never countenanced communalism, you have all your life fought against it. My injunction to you is that as long as you live, see to it that communalism does not take root in the soil of Bangladesh. You should be clear in your minds as to your aims, namely, Nationalism, Democracy, Socialism and Secularism. If you are to build up a socialist economy,

---

must protect non-Bengalis); 115 (exploiters say Islam is in danger, but we are better Pakistanis than they); 20, 41, 57, 66, 72, 74, 79 (appeals to Allah).

9 English translation of speech of June 7, 1972 (Dacca: External Publicity Division, Ministry of Foreign Affairs, Government of the People's Republic of Bangladesh, 1972), pp. 16–17.

10 English translation of speech of January 18, 1974 (Dacca: Department of Publications, Ministry of Information and Broadcasting, Government of Bangladesh, 1974), p. 3.

you must become a fully trained socialist cadre. Only then will you be successful. Of course, there are many people who want to defeat the aims of a socialist economy, because they cannot accept socialism. They are adopting indirect methods to oppose it. You have to oppose all those who in the name of progress are spreading communalism. You have to organize people from village to village and carry out a campaign among them to explain your aims.[11]

The warning of the Prime Minister about resurgent communalism is but one of numerous signs that Muslim self-assertiveness is on the rise in Bangladesh once again after the disgrace of 1971. Other signs include: the specter of "Muslim Bangla," a vague opposition slogan roundly denounced by the Awami League in the election of 1973; the Prime Minister's pledges of solidarity with his Arab brethren, his pride in prohibition of alcohol, increased numbers of pilgrims to Mecca, and other tokens of Muslim piety; official and popular eagerness to participate in the Muslim summit meeting in Pakistan; rejoicing at the prospect of good relations with Pakistan, epitomized in the warm greeting given Prime Minister Bhutto; reports by foreigners of outspoken anti-Indian and potentially anti-Hindu sentiments being voiced at Muslim gatherings; arrest of an editor (amid public indignation at his effrontery) for printing a piece satirizing belief in God; organization by Maulana Bhasani of a movement that may be a direct challenge to the prohibition of political activity in the name of religion; and numerous private remarks to the effect that the honeymoon with India, advocacy of the offensive policy of secularism, and refusal to tap Muslim sentiments for the task of nation-building have been carried too far. I refer to those signs as Muslim self-assertiveness, rather than communalism, because it is not yet clear that all or most of this assertiveness is destined to crystalize in the narrow, exploitative, obscurantist communal mold. Some of this sentiment would probably never degenerate into communalism. On the other hand, one suspects that much of the sentiment is malleable enough to go into either communal or tolerant molds depending upon what circumstances and leadership prevail. It seems crucial, therefore, that Bangladesh leadership construe the principle of secularism/tolerance in ways that constructively guide this Muslim assertiveness and not in a way that alienates it and leads to an unintended communal backlash. In the final portion of this essay I shall return to the question of the risk of communalism in Muslim assertiveness that is evident despite the pillar of secularism/tolerance. But since the threat of communalism dominates but one horn of the fundamental dilemma lying behind the fourth pillar, it is appropriate to consider the other horn, namely, the problem of securing adequate popular commitment to a sense of national identity and to the national goals without appealing to Muslim solidarity and ideals.

II. Bengali Language and Culture: The Source of National Identity

The first and most basic of the four principles of state policy is nationalism. It is, according to the Constitution, "based on the unity and solidarity of the

---

11   *Ibid.*, p. 13.

Bangalee nation," which nation in turn derives its identity from "its language and culture." Selection of language and culture as the source of national identity is by no means arbitrary. The process whereby East Pakistanis gradually became aware of themselves as a people distinct from West Pakistanis may be traced in their ongoing struggle to maintain Bengali as a national language, to thwart external efforts to deform the language, and to keep open communication with the literary springs of Bengali literature in Indian West Bengal. The national holiday, the political ritual if you will, that has been observed most spontaneously and solemnly before liberation from Pakistan and afterwards is February 21, the anniversary of the killing of several young men in a demonstration in behalf of Bengali language. Language, blood and country became the emotive symbols of Bengali resistance. These symbols, and the issues which gave rise to them are such as to embrace Bengalis of any economic class, any occupation, any religion, or any community. It is particularly significant that in debate over the merits of Urdu and Bengali the Bengali champions by and large avoided arguing on the grounds urged by the champions of Urdu: namely, that Bengali was less suitable as a Pakistani language than Urdu, since the latter had a literature rich in Muslim compositions, was written in the sacred Arabic script, and drew much of its vocabulary from Arabic. Whether they felt sufficiently sure of themselves as Muslims to treat this line of argument as a red herring, or whether they were unsure of their capacity to argue the aptness of Bengali for Islam, they preferred to base their defense of Bengali on its intrinsic literary merit and, more fundamentally, on the grounds that it was their own language and as such part of their own being. The great Hindu authors of Bengali literature became parts of the heritage to be defended and the Hindu minority in East Pakistan found itself supporting the dominant Awami League. Despite the transcendence of communal and class differences in the struggle for autonomy, however, the Muslims of Bengal seem to have considered themselves Pakistanis until the ultimate clash in 1971 and to have been surprised and stunned when their Muslim brothers from West Pakistan turned on them so brutally in the spring of that year.

When the reign of terror broke out in March, the academic and literary advocates of Bengali language and literature (and, by extension, culture) were already seasoned polemicists. They served admirably in diplomatic and public relations roles. To the Indians, they could present a portrait of a Bangladesh that in stark contrast to Pakistan was not ideologically Islamic, was in fact quite secular, and by literary and cultural heritage was closely tied to the Indian Sanskritic tradition. To liberal and socialist sympathizers abroad, the same portrait was attractive and conveyed the hope that the plague of communal violence would not convulse the new republic that was to arise with worldwide assistance from the ravages of 1971. Bengali intellectuals themselves became symbols of civilized Bengali resistance to the regressive brutality of the Pakistani army. The coordinated murder of scores of intellectuals, including a number of writers and students of Bengali literature, furnished belated confirmation of the charge that Pakistan was engaged in selective genocide against the cultural elite of Bangladesh. That atrocity on December 14, 1971, two days before liberation, provided a final group of martyrs in the cause of language, blood, and country.

To a large extent the national portrait of Bangladesh had been drawn by the Awami League leadership and its academic and literary associates before the return from India. The responsibility for articulating and propagating the national portrait, that now had to become a recognizable national identity in which the populace at large could participate, fell in large measure upon the same academic and literary cadres, in addition, of course, to the political leaders themselves. Bengali departments of the universities were strained to furnish public speakers, to produce popular tracts, and to work out serious expositions of Bengali national identity as derivable from language and culture. The one institution that most totally joined the campaign was the Bengali Academy, which dates back some years to the point where it was conceded that Bengali would be a national language. The Academy was founded to advance the status of Bengali through research and publications. At first, it emphasized new editions of older Bengali Muslim authors and translation of Muslim texts into Bengali. Later, its emphasis shifted to more secular and contemporary interests. Since liberation, its scope of operations and physical plant have expanded markedly. In addition to its traditional research and publishing activities it now oversees writing the official history of the freedom struggle, controls the operations of the Bengali Development Board, organizes and hosts a continuous round of cultural events in which academics, creative writers and government officials expound upon Bengali culture to sophisticated audiences, and even teaches Bengali clerks how to use the new German-made typewriters with Bengali script. The Bengali Academy is thus the main government agency for articulating the official view of Bengali national identity as derived from Bengali language and culture. The press, radio, television, cinema and, as always, the politicians carry the message to the populace at large. Is this enough to instill a nationwide sense of Bangladesh identity and commitment to its goals?

There are at least two basic reasons for doubting that language and culture are sufficient sources for an emotionally and cognitively adequate sense of national identity and purpose: their restricted emotional appeal; and the ambiguity of their boundary and content. It is one thing to rally an entire people in defense of their language (which implicates their livelihood and self-esteem) when that language is really in jeopardy. It is quite another thing to maintain passionate concern for the richness of a literature and culture long after the threat to the basic language has passed. As most Bengalis do not read, they may be respectful of the name of Rabindranath Tagore, but they can hardly be expected to build their private or corporate lives around him, as students of Bengali literature might be inclined to do. Even less, I suspect, can they identify with sophisticated contemporary poets and writers. Faced with staggering problems in economic, social, political, and religious life, the typical peasants and laborers of Bangladesh cannot live by language and culture alone. They need rice, and a palpable focus of solidarity, trust and direction.

The ambiguities of "language and culture" appear most sharply when one looks for the demographic boundary of the Bengali nation which is said to derive its identity from them. Are the fifty million Bengali speakers in India part of the Bengali nation? If not, why not? Is *de facto* Bangladesh only the core of a nation awaiting completion by its remaining half? If so, would the greater Bangladesh be an independent state or a member of the Indian union? The repercussions of either prospect could be explosive in India and Bangladesh if seriously espoused; yet removal of the map from the flag of Bangladesh and designation of its citizens officially by the generic name "Bangalee" in the Constitution do nothing to relieve the ambiguity. Presumably, the ambiguity is tolerated rather than intended. The alternative would be to propose an East Bengali culture and language which would almost surely take on the appearance of Muslim Bengali culture and language, something the Awami League does not want to encourage.

The ambiguities over who make up the Bengali nation are related to ambiguities in the concepts of Bengali language and culture themselves. Three basic models of Bengali language and culture occur to the reader of the Bangladesh Constitution, though the Constitution gives no indication of which is intended. These are the regional East Bengali model in which Muslim elements along with folk and dialectal ones would be conspicuous though embedded in a pan-Bengali matrix; a pan-Bengali model which would confront Bangladesh with the full gamut of complexity of Bengali language and culture – traditional and modern, eastern and western Bengali, Hindu and Muslim, sophisticated and folk; and an idealized extrapolation of what is judged most essential or desirable in Bengali language and culture.

The first model, the East Bengali regional one, has the advantage of being familiar to the citizens of Bangladesh. But it would accentuate the Muslim contributions to Bengali culture and the Arabic-Persian impact upon vocabulary. To espouse it would be tantamount to acceding to one of the fall-back positions of Pakistani foes of Bengali, to allow East Pakistanis to use Bengali provided they developed it away from the Sanskritic and toward the Urdu-Arabic-Persian tradition. This model seems to have been rejected in practice, if not explicitly. Literature by Muslims on Muslim themes is not receiving very much attention in Bengali departments at present. Enthusiasm for the classics of Bengali literature by Hindu authors is running high. Where there is a choice among synonyms, the one deriving from Sanskrit is usually preferred to the one deriving via Urdu from Arabic or Persian. Good Bengali style is modeled upon that of the Calcutta standard Bengali.

It is apparent also, though not quite so clearly, that the prevailing model is not the full unedited panorama of Bengali language and culture. While it is true that writers from all communities and regions are treated, texts with a narrow communal scope are passed over or dismissed with disapproval. Texts that are obviously religious – and such texts dominated Bengali literature until the nineteenth century – tend to be passed over, and texts with a religious level of significance but written in an idiom that can be read in strictly secular or humanistic terms tend to be interpreted exclusively on the latter level. Tribal rituals and the yogic songs of esoteric Bauls are treated as integral to Bengali culture, while explicitly Muslim, Hindu or Christian rituals and prayers usually are not. Historical analyses of Bengali language and culture tend to minimize both the Sanskritic and the Arabic-Persian contributions, though this can put the analyst in the awkward position of nearly identifying the Bengali with remnants of tribal and folk culture. The two great traditions just mentioned are not embraced enthusiastically because of the predominance of traditional religious concerns, the Brahmanic Hindu and the Muslim, respectively, in each. The pattern of acceptance and rejection that seems to be at work in current Bengali literary and cultural studies suggests that the third model of Bengali language and culture, some idealized extrapolation, is intended.

The ideal pattern that seems to underlie current interpretations of language and culture in Bangladesh may be characterized as Bengali aesthetic humanism. The Bengali aspect is evident enough from incessant reminders that it is our own Bengali language, our country, our cultural forms that are of value in themselves. There is relatively little appeal to universal standards to justify what is affirmed to be of great value in and of itself. The aesthetic emphasis is perhaps inevitable with so many creative writers and students of literature engaged in the interpretation of language and culture, but even foreign observers have noted frequently the unusually high priority which the aesthetic, particularly an emotionally expressive aesthetic, quality enjoys in Bengali life. This is by no means peculiar to East Bengal or Bangladesh. The third characteristic of the ideal pattern is its humanism, which rests in implied though not explicit tension with both theism and materialism. The fascination of Bangladesh scholars with Lalan Shah and other Bauls who sing of the man in the heart and with Rabindranath Tagore, whose *Religion of Man* expresses a very spiritual humanism, is indicative of this, as is the general pattern of acceptance and dismissal running through Bangladesh criticism of Bengali language and culture.

One line of poetry that a number of persons quoted to me illustrates this humanistic stress quite well. It is attributed to one Caṇḍī-dās a fifteenth century esoteric Vaiṣṇava, spiritually enamoured of a low-caste woman. He admonishes us to reverence the human being for there is nothing higher. The ideal is an attractive one and with suitable modifications need not be incompatible with the more humane tendencies within Muslim, Hindu, Christian and Buddhist traditions, as well as with agnostic and atheistic forms of humanism. For centuries, if not millenia, this humanistic strand has run through Bengali culture mellowing the religious traditions and political regimes that have played upon one another in the complex pluralistic history of Bengal. But one point that should not be overlooked is that most, if not all, of the individuals whose humanistic utterances have found favor with the Bengali people have been, as far as can be determined, deeply religious men (be they theists, tantric yogis, monists or adherents to some other form of spiritual discipline). Even those whose spiritual discipline seems to have been esoteric and unorthodox usually managed to express themselves in ways that the more orthodox could appreciate and approve. Whether we call this tack dissembling, polyvalent symbolizing of the ineffable, or something else, it is a flexibility which enabled the spokesmen of humanism in Bengali history to serve as agents of renovation within their respective religious traditions. They did not become alienated from the mainstreams of Hindu or Muslim symbolism.

Contemporary advocates of Bengali aesthetic humanism, by way of contrast, seem for the most part to be hesitant to articulate their humanistic faith, and, I suspect, in many cases their private faith in some communion of the human with the divine, with the traditional symbolism of Muslims or Hindus. It is by no means a problem exclusive to Bangladesh that persons exposed to the manifold demands of modern life often are stymied when it comes to integrating their secular humanistic insights and values with the values and symbolism of an inherited religious tradition. But the fact of that difficulty in integrating sectors of a person's values and symbolism suggests caution in offering as the paradigm of national identity a cultural ideal that heretofore has been only one strand, though a very significant one, of a complex culture anchored in two traditional religious systems. It is conceivable that an immensely creative cultural renaissance could transform what had been a distinctive trait within a pluralistic traditional Bengali culture into the controlling paradigm of a more unified and secular modern Bengali culture. I suspect that this is what a number of devotees of Bengali culture hope or think is coming to pass, though modesty and some ambiguity about what secular traditional Bengali culture has been tend to mute such heroic expectations. It may be my own insensitivity, but I do not see a renaissance of such proportions taking place at the moment.

It is conceivable also that the aesthetic humanistic strand of Bengali culture could entwine effectively with some other modern ideological systems that might replace the traditional religious systems. Socialism, revolution, and economic development come to mind as possible foci of widespread popular commitment somewhat analogous to traditional religious commitment. But such alternatives are at present possibilities, not actualities. As the *First Five Year Plan* says of socialism, it is "a vision and a dream." Furthermore, the advocates of Bengali aesthetic humanism seem to be divided among themselves when it comes to religious or ideological commitments which might coalesce with aesthetic humanism, some advocating socialism, some revolution; some are quite comfortable with secular liberalism, some remaining confident of the traditional religious paths. There does not seem to be much chance at the moment that the ancient Bengali ideal of aesthetic humanism will be able to recreate all of Bengali culture in its own image and likeness, nor that it will fuse decisively with any new ideological focus of meaning and solidarity. Furthermore, the impact of the official endorsement of Bengali aesthetic humanism is blunted and dissipated to some extent because its advocates are not always clear in showing that it is this ideal extrapolation and not the pluralistic Bengali culture as a whole that is to define the character of Bengali national identity.

If the foregoing contention is correct, i.e., that Bengali language and culture are not apt to engender a vibrant sense of national identity and purpose because of limited emotional appeal and ambiguities of boundary and content, is it necessarily a bad thing? Cannot Bangladesh, like Britain of old, just muddle through? Maybe it can. The Bengali people are used to disappointments and poor leadership. They really do not ask for much, though they have a way of losing patience eventually and reacting passionately when they do. When compounded with endemic poverty, pervasive mistrust, glaring incompetence, and persistent rumors of corruption, any further deterioration in morale due to inept handling of the symbolic resources of the people could be damaging. The last thing Bangladesh needs is more stagnation due to paralysis at the religious level, the level of valuing most intensively and most comprehensively. Since economic and demographic problems will grow ever more severe in the face of stagnation, eventually erupting into disaster, it is imperative that present Bangladesh leadership, in government and private life, come to terms with the religious level problems affecting the national identity and purpose of Bangladesh.

III. Secularism in Relation to the Risk of Communalism

The fundamental dilemma lying behind the fourth pillar of the Constitution of Bangladesh is that of stimulating adequate commitment to the nation and its goals without triggering a Muslim revival that might turn destructively communal. A dilemma specific to the pillar of secularism/tolerance itself is that of insulating the political process from communal tampering without offending Muslim sentiments by the very insulating mechanisms. Since there is evidence that the effort to define national identity and purpose without recourse to Muslim solidarity and ideals is not going to stimulate national morale to an adequate degree, it is appropriate to inquire more closely into the actual risk of destructive communalism in the current phenomenon of Muslim assertiveness in officially secular/tolerant Bangladesh.

How great is the risk of Muslim assertiveness turning communal in the pejorative sense of the term? Any definitive answer is out of the question, but certain observations may help place the question in focus and may suggest avenues of further investigation. Some historical considerations are in order at the outset. The three most powerful political movements of the nineteenth and twentieth centuries having their roots and their leadership among the Muslims of East Bengal are the Farā'izī movement of Haji Shariat Allah and Dudu Miyan in the early-middle nineteenth century, the Krishak Praja Party of A. K. Fazlur Huq in the second quarter of the twentieth century, and the Awami League of Shaheed Suhrawardy and Sheikh Mujibur Rahman. The first of these grew out of a religious revival but took on the form of organized secret resistance to those landlords who were exploiting their peasants. Despite the fact that the landlords were Hindus and the peasants usually Muslims, the Farā'izī movement did not turn into a generally anti-Hindu communal entity, although it did generate a sense of corporate identity among Muslim peasants and a sense of class interest that in all probability prepared the ground for Bengali Muslim advocacy of partition of Bengal and separation from India in the succeeding century. Neither the Krishak Praja Party nor the Awami League embraced religious reform, nor formulated its political policies in Muslim terms. Both have included Hindu members, but each was clearly a political instrument formed by and of East Bengali Muslims. More communal parties challenged the KPP and the AL, but apart from the all-Indian demand by Muslims for a separate state in 1947, such challenges have been rejected by Bengali Muslim voters in favor of the more secular and tolerant, but still overwhelmingly Muslim, parties.

Lying behind the movements and parties is the history of a relatively stable *modus vivendi* between Muslims and Hindus in rural Bengal. The hagiographical literature of the sixteenth century Vaiṣṇavas bears this out, as do sources for more recent periods. The history of accommodation between Muslims and Hindus in Bengal is in marked contrast with the history of Muslim-Sikh and Muslim-Maratha conflict in north and west India. The *modus vivendi* was upset by the loss of Muslim power to the British, competition for jobs by rising Hindu and Muslim middle classes, partition and reunification of Bengal, and the prospect of an independent democratic India where the Muslims would be a relatively weak minority. The violence of 1947 eventually affected Bengali Muslims and Hindus, but only after communal disturbances had gotten out of hand elsewhere in India and among the non-Bengalis resident in Calcutta. Memories of the violence of 1947 and of subsequent communal harassment of Hindus in East Pakistan have undermined the traditional solidarity of Hindus and Muslims in rural Bengal, who do share the same language and much of the same culture. How much of the harassment of Hindus in Pakistan was instigated by Muslim zealots who had migrated to East Pakistan and how much by native Bengali Muslims I do not know. In the atrocities of 1971 the pattern seems to have been encouragement by the non-Bengali regime of zealots and criminals, most of whom were native Bengalis, but atypical ones. In any case, some ten million Hindus are still living in Bangladesh, surviving if not prospering, reasonably safe if not free from anxiety. The major sources of irritation between Hindus and Muslims seem to have been removed in the course of separation from India and separation from Pakistan. Bengali Muslims are at last really in control of their own country. The Hindus and other minorities pose no real threat to them. With much of the world's humanitarian concern still directed toward Bangladesh and with India as a possible champion of the minorities all too close at hand, it is difficult to imagine any reasonable and responsible regime in Bangladesh instigating or condoning major harassment of the minorities. It is both good Muslim law and standard Muslim practice when in power to treat minorities with decency. The danger lies in the possibility of breakdown of law and order, when a regime is not securely in power, i.e., in times of severe crisis, especially if hostility toward India should dominate any such crisis.

Another source of perspective for assessing Muslim assertiveness in Bangladesh is the literary and intellectual history of Bengali Muslims. Here the preponderance of precedent lies on the side of responsible and humane relationships with non-Muslims. Conservative writers stressed divine justice and *noblesse oblige*; progressive writers added liberal humanistic reasons for magnanimous treatment of non-Muslims. The very fact that in the late nineteenth century, or the early twentieth, a Bengali Muslim chose to write in Bengali at all (rather than in Urdu, Persian or English) was a gesture of solidarity with non-Muslim Bengalis, for which gesture many were criticized by those who considered Bengali a Hindu language permeated with polytheism. It is ironic that some of these pioneers of modern Bengali Muslim literature, persons who had to grapple with some of the same problems of relating modernity and traditional faith as trouble many of us today, tend to be passed over in the current expositions of Bengali identity derived from language and culture. Although those Muslims who chose to make modern Bengali a medium for Muslim thought and literature were not the dominant force among the Muslims of their day (late nineteenth and early twentieth centuries), and even though some of them pulled back from their more liberal irenic posture in the face of rebuffs by Hindus from whom they had expected acceptance, still theirs is an encouraging precedent for the kind of Muslim self-consciousness that develops when Bengali Muslims can disentangle themselves intellectually from externally engendered crises. It would seem to be most indicative of the character of the present Muslim assertiveness, whether it attracts a leadership seriously concerned about examining the meaning of being Muslim and Bengali or whether it falls into the hands of those concerned only with managing and exploiting the threats and crises of the moment.

Present professional leadership of Bengali Muslims in religious and communal matters is generally of poor calibre, making it hazardous to anticipate the direction Muslim assertiveness will take. The members of the *ulema* who are highly regarded in the strictly traditional disciplines are few. Those who combine traditional expertise and appreciation of the modern world are exceedingly rare. Those *pirs* (spiritual advisers) who have not been disgraced by collaboration with the Pakistanis have not as yet shown an inclination for national ministry, as far as I know. The *maulanas* who staff the lower *madrasa* schools are handicapped by an outdated training and resistance to fundamental change. Many of the *maulanas* also were compromised by collaboration, but as a class they still command the respect of much of the rural Muslim population of Bangladesh. On such matters as family planning and altering the role of women their combined influence can have serious impact upon the developmental programmes of the Government. The best minds among the Bengali Muslims have not gone into the strictly Muslim professions, with rare exceptions. Thus one can appreciate the Prime Minister's candid remark that his people "can be misled more easily in the name of religion than by any other means."

The paucity of talent for constructive national leadership among the professional Muslims suggests that actual leadership of any movement of Muslim renovation that is more than *ad hoc* reaction to real or imagined threats will come from Muslim laymen. This could well mean return to the exploitation of Islam by shrewd and unscrupulous interests. However, it could also mean the emergence of conscientious Muslim laymen in a concerted effort to direct Muslim self-consciousness into constructive channels. This has happened before among Bengali Muslims, and with significant results. There are presently in Bangladesh a number of intelligent and respected individuals who have written ably on the relationship between traditional faith and life in the modern world. Before the Urdu-Bengali conflict distorted the intellectual and literary scenes a number of Bengali poets and authors were inspired to write as Muslims, to probe what it can mean to be human, Bengali and Muslim. It could happen again. The universities have able scholars in Bengali, history, Islamic history and other departments who have examined the Muslim aspects of life in what is now Bangladesh. Even if such a constructive movement of Muslim renovation were to crystalize out of the inchoate assertiveness of Bengali Muslims, it might have to face challenges to its leadership from incompetent and poorly disposed laymen and perhaps from the conservative professional *ulema* and *maulanas*, or sections of them. One may speculate on the chances of its maintaining public confidence, as one may speculate on the appropriate governmental stance toward such a movement, but from this vantage point it would be sheer guesswork.

If such a movement of Muslim renovation were to come to fruition in Bangladesh, its achievements in rethinking the meaning of being Muslim in Bangladesh in the modern world could well have impact upon Muslim developments in other countries. Since Bangladesh is comparatively secular, tolerant and pluralistic to begin with, it would seem probable that more fundamental breakthroughs in renewal of Muslim life could be arrived at there than would be likely in other more traditional or ideologically narrow countries where Muslims are in the majority. Leaving aside direct political action, there are countless ways in which Muslims could engage more devotedly than they have in works of nursing, education, cooperatives, and other unprofitable but essential services. Stimulation of Muslim motivation for such service of neighbour and nation is one of the most direct outcomes that a constructive renovation of Muslim life could bring. This need not, though it might, require alteration of the Constitution's affirmation of secularism/tolerance, but clearly it would call for a change in how Bengalis think, talk, and feel about the meaning of being Muslim in relation to national identity and purpose.

Summary and Conclusion

Even though the rigor of the Constitution's exclusion of religion from the political realm and the fervor of the *First Five-Year Plan*'s espousal of secularism hint at a more radical and possibly ideological construction of the concept of secularism/tolerance than do the statements of the Prime Minister, the feasibility of any radical secularization of Bangladesh is by this time minimal. The reassertiveness of Muslims as Muslims and the absence of an effective organizational instrument for effecting any radical secularization rule it out. Still there has been a general inhibition thus far against public discussion of traditional Islam, or Islamic ideals, in the context of public policy and national identity. In view of stagnating morale and the limited emotive and cognitive adequacy of Bengali language and culture alone as sources for national identity and purpose, pressure is building up for a more explicit appeal to Muslim solidarity and ideals to make up what is wanting. Other sources of popular ideological commitment, such as socialism, revolution and development, are not at present broadly and deeply enough realized to provide nationwide religious level commitment to the task of nation-building.

There is uncertainty and risk in encouraging explicit recourse to Muslim solidarity and Muslim ideals in view of the communalism recently exhibited during the Pakistani regime and the unprogressive professional Muslim leadership in Bangladesh. However, the long term history of Bengali Muslims shows considerable resistance to communal abuse, even amid energetic movements of religious and political renovation. Recent history, dominated by the Indo-Pakistani conflicts and intrusion into Bengali Muslim affairs by partisans of Urdu, has not been so encouraging, and is apt to leave Hindus in Bangladesh and India less confident of Bengali Muslim responsibility than in the new circumstances they might be. There are Bengali Muslim laymen respected for genuine concern and for expertise in Islamic matters who could provide responsible guidance in any movement for renovation of Muslim life in Bangladesh. Refusal of Bangladesh political leadership to give scope to those non-communalists desiring to channel Muslim assertiveness into constructive channels and the failure to modify or spell out the meaning of secularism/tolerance in ways less discouraging to Muslim self-consciousness, are apt to bring further deterioration of national morale and revival of the very communalism the fourth pillar is intended to eliminate.

Lest any revision of the fourth pillar be viewed as unworthy capitulation to reactionary pressures, the observation of a noted scholar writing at the time of Pakistan's emergence a generation ago is worthy of reflection.

> Given the fact that it is a democracy (formally) and that the great majority of its citizens are Muslims, it must, virtually, pursue Islamic ideals or no ideals at all. For practical purposes, the alternative to the Islamic state is complacency or corruption.[12]

---

12   Wilfred Cantwell Smith, *Pakistan as an Islamic State* (preliminary draft) (1951, rpt. Lahore: Sh. Muhammad Ashraf, 1962), p. 86.

Bangladesh is not Pakistan. It is more secular, more pluralistic, and more tolerant in its history than the region that has become Pakistan. It has had a generation of bad experience with what was presented as an Islamic state. Yet the basic point, appropriately nuanced, still holds true, I think. So long as the great majority of its citizens think of themselves as Muslims as well as Bengalis, Bangladesh must pursue Muslim ideals as well as Bengali ones, if it is to pursue any ideals wholeheartedly. To pursue its Muslim and its Bengali ideals constructively and without inner conflict Bangladesh may have to develop mechanisms peculiar to itself. But to be able to discover and implement such mechanisms the people of Bangladesh, and especially their leaders in public and private affairs may have to face squarely difficult problems and make difficult choices at the level of religious valuing. Political maneuvering and economic planning alone are not apt to propel the people of Bangladesh to a vibrant and humane experience of national identity and national purpose.[13]

13 For further discussion of Bengali Muslim thought in the British period and for a valuable bibliography on Bengali Muslim thought from the medieval period to the present see Mahmud Shah Qureshi, *Étude sur l'Evolution Intellectuelle ches les Musulmans du Bengale, 1857–1947* (Paris and the Hague: Mouton & Co., 1971).

This essay was written prior to the assassination of Sheikh Mujibur Rahman.

Land, Personhood, and Sorcery in a Sinhalese Village[1]

A. J. SELVADURAI

San Diego State University, San Diego, U.S.A.

THIS PAPER is about people, land, and land disputes in a Sinhalese village in the Western Province of Sri Lanka. Specifically, the paper addresses the problem of what land disputes are about. I intend to demonstrate that land disputes are about social relationships, and that who owns what piece of land is only a way of talking about the social relationship. In order to demonstrate my hypothesis data on land tenure and land disputes will be presented and then subjected to a cultural analysis. What is at issue is the *meaning*, culturally defined, of land, of persons, and of the relationship between them. We shall look at the Sinhalese definition both of personhood and of land, and then data will be presented on two land disputes and examined in the light of the notion of personhood.

Some recent developments in cultural anthropology (see Geertz 1966, Guemple 1974, and Schneider 1968, for example) have indicated that the concept of the person is a key explanatory variable in sociocultural analysis. In keeping with this orientation I shall treat "the person" as a conceptual construct distinct from the individual on-the-ground.[2]

The person is defined in Sinhalese peasant society with reference to two imageless abstractions, namely "whole" and "part", on the basis of which it is possible to distinguish two categories of persons: "whole persons" and "part persons". In the idiom of the village community, a whole person is designated as a "citizen" of the village, and the part person as an "outsider". Each kind of person enjoys a particular kind of kinship status and a particular set of rights, duties and privileges in relation to land.

A dispute over land represents the claim of a part person for the rights of

---

1 I conducted the research, on which this paper is based, during the year 1971–72 while I was attached to the academic staff of the University of Sri Lanka, Peradeniya. The data were originally collected for a doctoral dissertation. I owe thanks to several colleagues: Gananath Obeyesekere, then Chairman of the Department of Sociology at Peradeniya, for his helpful comments during my period of research, Simon Ottenberg for his useful insights, and Michael Lieber for the encouragement given in adopting the theoretical orientation I have used here, and for help in preparing this paper for publication.

2 Schneider (1973) makes a like distinction between "the kinsman as person" and "the person as kinsman".

a whole person. The claim for equal land rights, regardless of the status differences between citizens and outsiders, is validated by a legal tradition and legal institutions brought into existence as a result of colonial rule. The law is egalitarian and contractual in nature, and all persons are existentially equal and are identical before the law. Thus, two conflicting definitions of the person – one within, and the other outside the village – need to be taken into consideration.

The emphasis on the cultural (conceptual) framework within which disputes are contained is a departure from previous studies of land disputes in Sinhalese peasant society. In particular, this paper takes issue with the conclusions arrived at by Leach in his study of a peasant community in another part of the island: "In the end, it seemed to me that all the complicated arguments about... kinship status amounted to a way of talking about a quarrel over land and water" (1968:310). In Leach's view, land and water are simply material resources (i.e., objects), and disputes over them reflect the primacy of "economic" over ideological factors.

The position taken in this paper is that land is principally a set of relations which define the rights, duties and privileges between persons with respect to the soil. Land, as a concept distinct from the soil, also serves in disputes as a vehicle through which individuals convey important meanings to one another.

Some aspects of disputes indicate that more than simple "economic" concerns are at issue. For instance, most disputes are conducted at the expense of considerable amounts of time, money and labor, which more often than not, exceed the material (cash) value of the land. Two factors underlie this apparent economic irrationality. One is that villagers regard land as having a kind of durability and permanence which is not shared by goods such as cash, houses, and garden trees. Informants would state, for example, that "land would continue to exist as long as the planet earth exists." Any investment in land is, thus, a relatively safe and enduring one. Secondly, the continuity of land also stands for the continuity of the person and kinship; thus, land, kinship, time and person are inextricably intertwined to form a single relational scheme.

The relationship between disputes and the scheme of relations defining the person is also reflected in the fact that disputes vary significantly in content and outcome according to the categories of person involved. Whereas disputes among citizens are usually settled within a framework of amity and consensus, disputes between citizens and outsiders invariably end up in courts of law and/or tend to remain unsettled for relatively long periods.[3]

A critical difference between the two types of disputes is the occurrence of sorcery accusations and suspicions when the dispute involves citizens and out-

---

3   The focus of a dispute is a plot of land, and the dispute will involve more than one individual or household. Out of a total of 9 plots, over which disputes have taken place within the last 25 years, 6 plots involved citizens and outsiders; the remainder were concerning citizens. Five out of the 6 "disputes" between citizens and outsiders were taken to court for settlement, out of which 2 have been settled. Again, out of these 6 disputes, 4 contained sorcery accusations or suspicions of sorcery; in 2 there was physical violence, as well.

siders. In this context, sorcery is not merely a regulatory mechanism, being that it maintains the traditional system, but it is also a statement of the conceptual boundaries between citizens and outsiders as different categories of persons.

Given the limitations of space, I shall only outline the salient features of the village setting, of the kinship structure, and of the system of rights in relation to land (for additional ethnographic details see Selvadurai 1973). Two land disputes will be presented in detail and in support of the points made above; these two examples have been selected from a total of nine disputes which have taken place within the last twenty-five years.

Description

Setting

The village of Mulgama[4] is situated on the northern boundary of the Western Province of Sri Lanka; the Province is a part of the ecological area known as the Wet Zone which has an annual average rainfall of over eighty inches. The village population of roughly 2000 persons (350 households) are Sinhalese Buddhists, and they belong to the "farmer" (goigama) caste. The villagers are primarily subsistence paddy cultivators; a few are engaged in other occupations ranging from employment in government service to hired agricultural labor. Villagers cultivate paddy during two seasons of the year: maha (from September through January) and yala (from April through August), the land area used for paddy cultivation being about 163 acres. They use 487 acres for residence and for the cultivation of garden crops such as rubber, coconut and vegetables.[5]

The village is not an isolated geographic, social or political entity. A network of roads and footpaths connects the village with surrounding villages, and a main road, serviced by a public transport system, connects the village with two townships, Horana and Padukka, both of which are situated about seven miles away. Several administrative and judicial agencies of the central government such as the District Revenue Office[6], the District Courts[7], the

---

4 "Mulgama" is a pseudonym.
5 Out of a sample of 25 households 20% owned less than half an acre, and 56% owned up to 2 acres. The remainder owned between 2.75 and 25 acres. Note that the extents owned include both paddy and highland.
6 Each District Revenue Office has 5 Divisions under its supervision. Each Division is comprised of several villages and is managed by a Village Council made up of representatives elected by the villagers.
7 The District Court handles cases which the local Conciliation Board cannot settle. The Conciliation Boards were instituted by the central government to arbitrate on disputes at the village-level so that villagers may be spared the costs and trouble incurred once they take a dispute to the District Court. However, as will be seen in the description of land disputes, the make-up of each judicial body determines the outcome of judicial procedure in each. The District Court is presided by impartial judges appointed by the Ministry of Justice, whereas the appointments to the Board are made on the basis of

local police station and an Agrarian Office[8] are situated in Horana. Padukka holds a fair once a week where agricultural products are bought and sold. From these two townships villagers have access to the city of Colombo and to other towns in the vicinity.

Kinship, Land and Personhood

Though Mulgama is a one-caste community, its residents fall into two hierarchically ranked, terminological categories, "citizen" and "outsider", which signify the status of individuals in a larger conceptual scheme. The formal units of this scheme can be subsumed under the terms "whole" and "part". They define the relations which obtain among citizens and outsiders with respect to kinship and property. Briefly stated, whole persons are those who claim citizenship in the village by virtue of membership in a named agnatic category called a *vasagama*. They share the whole blood of the *vasagama* ancestor and they have full or whole rights to the use and ownership of land. By contrast, part persons are those who cannot claim citizenship in the village, who remain outsiders by virtue of membership in other *vasagam* (plural of *vasagama*), who are related to the citizens by marriage and not by blood, and who do not have full rights to the use and ownership of land.

The *vasagama* is a named, exogamous category of agnates; membership in this category is represented in the use of a particular surname[9] which is transmitted through males.[10] Though there are persons having membership in about thirty different *vasagam* in the village, the members of only one *vasagama*, comprising roughly half the village population, qualify for citizenship. Their dominant position is based on the claim that their ancestor was the first to settle the village, an event which is said to have taken place sometime during the latter half of the eighteenth century. According to villagers, that ancestor had received land from the Dutch colonial government of the time in return for services he performed as a village headman. He had also assumed an honorific surname which his descendants continue to use today.[11]

---

recommendations of the local Member of Parliament who invariably is influenced by kinship, caste or political considerations.

8 The Agrarian Office supervises and funds the village-level body known as the Cultivation Committee which handles disputes among farmers, collects statistics on yields, and acts as an instrument for agricultural extension.

9 A person has two names, namely his surname and his personal name. For example, the full name of Somapala, a personal name, is Samarakoon Achige Somapala; the suffix *ge* ("of") indicates that he is a member of a category of agnates using the surname, Samarakoon Achi.

0 On rare occasions a female will give her surname to her children if the latter have no legitimate father. In the three instances where this has taken place in Mulgama, her agnates consider the children as "low" in status, and ostracize them from marriage ceremonies. Agnates will mete out the same punishment to members of the same *vasagama* who have intermarried.

11 Informants refer to the existence of a Dutch land record of about 1770 in support of this claim. This record is available in the Archives in Colombo, and two individuals in the village have Sinhalese translations of it.

Besides the historical association of the surname with land and with rights of residence it is used today for several different purposes. In informal discourse, informants use it to distinguish a citizen from an outsider; in making the distinction they will refer to the fact that the outsider has a different surname. Villagers also use the surname when registering a birth, marriage or death, when making deeds or wills, or when making written applications for jobs.

In addition to the sharing of a surname, members of a *vasagama* also form a single category of blood relations. This is based on the assumption that, like surnames, blood is transmitted by the male parent in full (via his semen), whereas blood is transmitted in part by the female parent (via her milk). The ideology of blood relationship affirms, on the one hand, the affinal relationship between citizens and outsiders, for the latter are either uxorilocally resident males or their descendants. On the other hand, the ideology makes a statement about the status of the affine as a person: if the sharing of blood of an ancestor is one attribute of the whole person, then the outsider is not a whole person (since females transmit blood only in part).

Citizenship also implies a particular set of rights and privileges with regard to land. The differences between the rights of citizens as opposed to rights of outsiders again rest on the distinction between males and females, and between the rights of each sex. That is, though male and female children inherit equal shares in the parental property, ideally only males are entitled to both rights of ownership and rights of use; females own shares in land, but their use rights are subordinate to the rights of their agnates.[12]

Ownership and use are distinguished terminologically. Ownership (*ayithiya*) means simply the ability to claim a share or shares in a given estate. Ownership of a share entitles a person (1) to use and enjoy it; (2) to transfer use by rent or lease; (3) to transfer ownership *inter vivos* by sale or gift; (4) to reclaim use after a period of not using the land; and (5) to demand right-of-way. Whereas ownership refers to the ability or competence of a person with regard to rights in land, use (*buktiya*) refers to the actualization of this ability. Thus the term *buktiya* covers the following kinds of activities: (1) building a house and occupying it; (2) cultivating the land; (3) disposing of the produce from the land by direct consumption or by sale; and (4) pasturing cattle and gathering firewood. Again, unlike the term for ownership, *buktiya* is associated with actions that sustain and nourish the body: eating food, enjoying what is eaten, and deriving sustenance from food.

The prestige attached to virilocal residence for a female (*deega*) and the low prestige attached to uxorilocal residence for a male (*binna*) noted by all students of Sinhalese peasant society has meaning in the context of the different allocation of rights in land between males and females. That is, the normatively desired forms of residence for males and females endorse the ideal that the village be composed of a group of agnatic kin who own as well as use the land.

---

12   An out-resident female may activate her ownership rights by selling, mortgaging or leasing her share to a co-parcener. She may also demand a share of the harvest at the end of each season.

Out-marrying females will own shares but not use the village land, and in-marrying females will not have the ownership rights in, but may enjoy the shares of their spouses.[13]

Finally, whole/part relations also define the principles and methods underlying the use of a given estate. The fundamental premise is that co-parceners use the estate as an undivided whole, though each has a share in it. Thus, a share (*kotasa*, literally "a part of" a whole object) exists in relation to other shares. The primary duty of a co-parcener is that he refrain from separating his share from the whole either by erecting a fence or other boundary between his portion and the rest of the estate, or by having the estate partitioned through a court of law. There is also the expectation that each co-parcener should be able to use all parts of the estate. The operation of this principle varies in the actual uses of highland and paddyland. In the case of highland, the co-parceners usually divide the garden trees or the produce of the trees equally among themselves. In the case of paddyland, where there is considerable variation in the fertility of the soil, each co-parcener has access to the whole field by taking a turn cultivating both fertile and infertile parts.

Rights of Part-Persons

The normatively desired forms of marriage and residence do not occur in all individual instances. That is, not all females marry out; nor do all males reside patrilocally. Certain females continue to remain in the village either because of their attachment to parents, or because they do not have male siblings to inherit and use the parental land. These females may marry men who are willing to reside uxorilocally; the latter and their descendants constitute the ranks of outsiders of the village.

The rights of outsiders are by definition partial rights. The concept of incomplete or partial rights is conveyed by the term *adui* which is used to refer to outsiders as a kind of person, and to the rights of outsiders. First, the term has connotations of inequalities of status between two persons; thus, *adui* is used to refer to a person of a caste lower than the caste of the speaker. Secondly, the term is used to describe inequality in the allocation of a good.

The above meanings are conveyed in the way a female's agnates allocate land to her and to her spouse. For example, she usually receives the use of a portion of land which does not constitute her full share in the parental property. Agnates may also impose limits on the exercise of her use rights by preventing her from using the produce of garden trees. Thus, deviations from the norm that females should marry out are re-interpreted in terms of the larger scheme of conceptual relations. Rights of females and their spouses remain partial rights although the former have remained resident.

---

13 The principle of "community of property between spouses" introduced through Roman-Dutch law has modified this to a considerable extent. I observed only two instances where in-marrying females have utilized the principle to re-allocate the shares of their spouses after the latters' deaths. Both females have given their shares to their children.

Land Disputes

Land disputes center around the limitations that agnates have imposed on the exercise of use rights of females. An outsider and/or his spouse will precipitate a dispute by claiming the rights of a citizen, or, in other words, by claiming a change from partial to full personhood. The claim for equality of rights and of status stems from the recognition (on the part of citizen and outsider) that there is a system of laws and courts of law outside the village which define the person and his rights differently. That is, all persons stand equal and have equal rights before the law. On the one hand, the law is something alien and outside the village. With regard to inheritance, the law is Roman-Dutch in origin, and it has subsequently been modified by British Common Law and by the Statutes of the British Parliament. Roman-Dutch law was introduced by the British colonial government (1815 to 1948) and has been in existence since the 1870's. On the other hand, the law of the courts (*nithiya*) is distinct from the unwritten rules and obligations (*yuthukam*) among kinsmen.

The aspect of the law relevant to our purposes is its recognition that both sexes have equal claims where inheritance and exercise of use rights are concerned. For example, in the case of intestate inheritance "...children succeed equally... males and females alike" (Lee 1953:407). Nor is there any provision in the law imposing limits on or preventing females from exercising use rights.

Another aspect related to land disputes is that the law provides for the partition of a given estate according to shares claimed in court. Thus, an outsider may precipitate a dispute in the hope of having a court of law separate his legal (if not legitimate) share from the whole estate.

Appeal to the principles and procedures of a court of law thereby constitutes not only a violation of expectations among kinsmen but also a state of disorder within an entire conceptual scheme. In a dispute, then, an outsider claims the rights of a citizen, a part person demands the status of a full person, and a co-parcener wishes to have a part of the estate separated from the whole.

Dispute No. 1

The disputants are J. Pubilis Singho, an uxorilocally resident male, and his wife's classificatory brothers[14], Coronis and Suaris, who are citizens of the village.

Pubilis' father had been a resident of a village on the northern boundary of Mulgama. Around 1906, he had purchased a share in a plot of land in Mulgama and had come to reside there. In 1930, Pubilis married Emi Nona and came to reside in her father-in-law's house which was situated towards the middle of the village. This plot of land, about 2 acres in extent, was divided into two portions by a road. In one portion was Emi Nona's parental household; the other portion was unused at this time (I shall refer to these two portions as A and B, respectively).

About 1940, the Village Council closed the existing road, and opened a new road about 10 yards west of the old one. Pubilis' father-in-law, who had been running a tea-shop in his house, moved his business from plot A to plot B, and constructed a tea-shop

---

14   Individuals of the same generation who are also members of the same *vasagama* address one another by the term for "sibling" (*sahodaraya* and *sahodari* for male and female siblings, respectively). Genealogically, Emi Nona is the daughter of Coronis' father's father's father's brother's son's son.

using an area of about 2 perches. Around 1942, Pubilis' father-in-law and his classificatory brother, Haramanis, together cleared the unused portion of plot B (which was about half an acre), and planted rubber trees. They enjoyed the produce of the trees in common. By 1947, both partners had died; the share of Pubilis' father-in-law devolved on his only child, Emi Nona, and that of Haramanis on his two sons, Coronis and Suaris. Pubilis managed the tea-shop and he continued to reside in portion A.

In 1953, Coronis adopted a course of action which became the immediate cause of the dispute. Without consulting his co-parcener, Emi Nona, he uprooted all rubber trees in which both had shares, and planted a new set of rubber trees using the entire half acre portion. Nor did he share the proceeds from the rubber trees with his co-parcener. Pubilis informed me that his wife did not challenge the action "because there was no able person in the household". (His father-in-law was survived by two females: Emi Nona and her mother. It is noteworthy that Pubilis did not consider himself an able person. The statement conveys clearly Pubilis' estimation of himself as an outsider, and as a person without full personhood since he had no shares in the land in question.)

Another set of events contributed to an escalation of the dispute. In 1953, Pubilis made plans to replace the house he was using with a brick-and-tile structure; the former house. made of wattle and daub, had gone decrepit. He tore the old house down, and moved with his wife and two children (a daughter of 18 years and a son of 16) into the tea-shop until the new house was built; by this time his wife's mother was not living. But the tea-shop was too small for the family, and they also needed space to construct a kitchen. The only way this could be done was by acquiring a portion of the land which Coronis now used.

Since Coronis and Emi Nona held the land in common, at least in theory if not in fact, the latter visited Coronis at his house and informed him that the area she used in portion B would be expanded to build a kitchen. Coronis had replied that she could not use any more land, and that "even if he lost all his wealth, she would not get an inch more." Coronis' stand was consistent with the principle that a female's right to use land should be subordinate to the rights of her agnates although, in addition to the area required for the kitchen (about half a perch), Emi Nona would only be using a mere two-and-a-half perches or 1/64th of an acre as opposed to the half acre used by Coronis. Her total share in portion B should be 1/4 acre, if she and Coronis inherited equally.

However, Emi Nona was not prepared to accept these limitations. Returning home from her visit she set fire to one of the rubber trees. (Her aggression was directed towards the rubber trees since they belonged to Coronis, but stood on land in which she had a joint interest.) Coronis filed a case in the Rural Courts[15] claiming damages for the tree. Meanwhile he cut a drain, about three feet broad, separating the tea-shop from the rest of the land, and thereby preventing the construction of a kitchen. Pubilis complained to the local police, and the Headman of the village held the inquiry. He advised Coronis to close the drain since it was an undivided estate, and the latter complied.

By now, Pubilis and his wife were no longer interested in getting land to construct a kitchen; they began to press Coronis for the full share of land. The previous event had validated the fact that Coronis held his rubber trees on land in which Emi Nona also had shares. But, Coronis would not consider this claim. In retaliation Pubilis and his son mutilated a larger number of the rubber trees; the year was 1956. Coronis fought back by complaining to the local police that Pubilis was growing *ganja* (a type of narcotic weed prohibited by law). The police found Pubilis innocent, and reprimanded the accuser. In the same year, the Rural Courts made a decision on the claim for damages that Coronis had made: the Courts asked Emi Nona to pay a fine of 25 rupees. On returning home from the courts, Pubilis and his son uprooted all the rubber trees. Coronis hired about fifty men from another village to construct a barbed-wire fence separating the tea-shop from the rest of the land. After the men left, Emi Nona and her son broke

---

15   At that time, the rural courts performed the same functions as do the Conciliation Boards today.

the fence down; Pubilis was away from home on that day. When Coronis heard of this, he came carrying a gun, abused Emi Nona and threatened to kill her. She snatched a sword lying in the house and struck at Coronis. He parried the blow with his gun, but the sword slid downwards injuring one of his fingers. He filed a case in the Police Courts[16]; the Courts found Emi Nona guilty of unprovoked assault (!), and imposed a fine of 20 rupees. Though about fifty villagers had witnessed the incident, not one came forward to give evidence. (Their refusal to do so conveys what they thought about the issue; in their view, Pubilis and his wife were in the wrong.) In 1960, Coronis brought down another group of men, barbwired the land, and planted a new set of rubber trees. Pubilis and his wife watched the event helplessly.

After this event Pubilis did not make a fuss for the next two years; his son described the period as one of "silence and defeat". Apparently, the superior resources of Coronis had prevailed. During this time Pubilis had recourse to another kind of 'power', namely that of sorcery. He brought down various ritual specialists from other villages to inflict some harm on his opponent, and spent a considerable amount of money doing so. In his estimation, sorcery has had some effect: today Coronis, who is about 55 years old, suffers from partial paralysis. When I questioned the latter, he stoutly denied that sorcery has had anything to do with his illness.

While these events were taking place, Coronis had transferred ownership of the rubber trees to his brother, Suaris. In 1962, the dispute again came into the open. Pubilis' son had been at the village store one evening. (The store serves as a community center where villagers gather to talk, exchange news and purchase their household goods.) Coronis had arrived, and a man named Obias had asked him whether there was any more trouble regarding the land. Coronis had denied with gusto. Pubilis' son felt that this was done to humiliate him; he came home and cut down several rubber trees. Suaris, the new owner, complained to the police, and the Police court ordered Pubilis' son to pay a fine of 80 rupees. After paying the fine he returned home and broke down the fence that Coronis had erected for the second time. Suaris complained to the police; the police took the offender into custody and allowed him to go on bail for the sum of 200 rupees. This time the case was taken up by the District Court; the judge advised Suaris not to enter the land until and unless he partitioned it through court. Suaris then filed a case in the same court claiming damages from Pubilis' son for having broken the fence down. The court dismissed the case with costs to the accused. Suaris appealed against this decision and won the appeal; Pubilis' son had to pay 200 rupees to Suaris.

Though the court instructed Suaris to file a partition case, he did not do so. Instead, he sold his share to another citizen, Obias. (If he had had the land partitioned, Emi Nona would have received her 'legitimate' share.) Obias continued the policy of using the entire plot disregarding the share of Emi Nona.

Around 1965, he began building a house in portion B. He also put up a fence around the plot replacing the one which Pubilis' son had torn down. The next day, Pubilis tore the fence down. Obias complained to the police; the Police Court warned Pubilis and advised Obias to have the land partitioned through the local Conciliation Board. He acted accordingly, and Pubilis and his family attended the hearing for partition. Both parties agreed on partition. On the following day, the Board members came to the village to divide up the land. However, Obias' political and kin connections with some of the Board members influenced the decision of the Board in his favor. The Board gave Emi Nona a strip of land, about 3 feet broad, comprising 1/8 of an acre, and gave the rest of the land to Obias. Though Emi Nona received a portion of land less than the share she claimed, she and her husband accepted this decision. Parenthetically, it may be added that though the one-fourth acre share he fought for was worth about 700 rupees in the open market, he spent over 1300 rupees in fines (325 rupees), in payments for lawyers (800 rupees) and in incidental expenditures (300 rupees) trying to obtain it!

---

16 The Police Courts are presided by the Police Magistrate; the Courts handle cases of theft, injury to persons or to property in which the Police have been involved.

By 1960, Pubilis had completed the new house, and he uses it today. He and his son still manage the teashop. Apart from this activity, he regards himself as a recluse. He practices meditation in the village Buddhist temple; he is virtually a "lay saint" (*upasaka*). When interviewed, he extolled the higher tenets of Buddhism: the impermanence of the secular world, the suffering that follows from attachment to it, and the necessity for withdrawal and for contemplation. He also participates in a ceremony called *gihi pirith,*, in which laymen chant sacred Buddhist texts in village homes to remove minor misfortunes and illnesses. However, his son indicated to me that, as far as he is concerned, the dispute is not settled, and that he was lying low since he does not wish to involve his parents in further trouble.

Dispute No. 2

The disputants are K. Sugathan, an uxorilocally resident male, and his wife's brothers, Guneris, Obias, Albin and Surabiyel, who are citizens of the village. Sugathan married Jane Nona, his real mother's brother's daughter. His father had come to Mulgama in 1920 to take care of a six acre plot of land which a resident of Mulgama had sold to a resident of another village. Sugathan's father subsequently married a descendant of the founding ancestor.

When he came to reside with his wife's brothers he occupied a portion of land, about a half-acre in extent, which was a part of a larger plot of 4 acres. Three households used the entire plot: Sugathan and his wife, his wife's father, and his wife's oldest brother. Her two other brothers who were unmarried at that time were living with their father; her only female sibling had gone out on marriage.

Sugathan informed me that he was using his mother's share in the plot, and his wife's brothers (i.e., mother's brother's sons) had raised no objections when they came into residence. Instead, they allowed him to use a portion of land smaller than his mother's full share to build a house and to grow a few garden trees. If the land was to devolve equally among Sugathan's mother and her two brothers, Sugathan would be using 1/3rd of 4 acres or 1 and 1/3 acres, whereas the portion he actually used was only half an acre.

In 1955, he decided to rebuild his house, which was a wattle-and-daub structure, and began to collect the materials for a brick-and-tile house. He communicated verbally to his wife's brothers that the area he was using was insufficient for the new house, and that he wanted a larger portion. The latter informed him that what Sugathan had was all he was going to get. He protested saying that he was entitled to two shares, namely, his mother's share of 1 and 1/3 acres, plus his wife's share of 1/6th of 1 and 1/3 acres or 1/8 acre; the total in acres would be 1 and 11/24 acres or roughly 1½ acres.

His wife approached her brothers and asked about her share. The latter replied that she had no rights in the land, since their father had willed all his shares in land to the sons excluding the two daughters. This claim proved to be untrue when I checked the Register of Lands for Mulgama. An entry for the year 1962 states that Poris had gifted all his shares in land to the sons "excluding undivided 1/6th share of an undivided 1 acre[17] of undivided 4 acres..." The undivided 1/6th acre which their father (Poris) had excluded was that of Sugathan's wife, Jane Nona. She corroborated this by informing me that at his deathbed Poris had informed her: "I have done a great wrong, but I have left a little for you in highland." She explained that her father had willed shares in paddy to the sons excluding the two daughters ("the great wrong" he referred to), but that he had left something for her in highland.

For about a year a verbal tug-of-war prevailed between Sugathan and his wife's brothers. The latter informed him finally that if he wanted to have the shares he claimed

---

17 The "undivided one acre" refers to the share of Sugathan's mother. It will be noticed that Poris had reduced her share from 1 and 1/3rd acres in making the deed; this indicates that he adhered to the principle that females who remained resident were not entitled to equal shares.

he would have to go to court. But another sequence of events prevented him from either going to court or building his house.

Around 1957, he had found employment as a night watchman in a rubber estate in the vicinity of Mulgama. In the early hours of one morning, he was doing his usual rounds through the estate when he saw what looked like a rabbit. He followed the creature and fired several shots at it with his gun. The creature was unharmed and went out of sight. He came home, ate the morning meal of rice, and an hour later he developed a high fever. A ritual specialist from Mulgama, who was called to cure him, attributed the illness to "the evil influence" of a demon known as Maha Sohona or "demon of the cemetery"; he identified the rabbit as a manifestation of this supernatural. The specialist tied charmed threads[18] on the patient, and the fever subsided. After about a year Sugathan began to complain of a loss of appetite. By the end of the year, 1958, he began to have spells of fainting during which he would babble, try to run out of the house, and to overpower those who restrained him. These fits would subside as soon as a ritual specialist tied charmed threads on him. About 1969, he injured his hand while working in the fields; the wound festered and he had to undergo surgery at the government hospital in Horana.

While he was hospitalized his wife consulted a diviner from a village in the vicinity. He revealed that someone had committed sorcery on the family, and that Sugathan had become the victim since his astrological period was not propitious.[19] When interviewed, Sugathan and his wife claimed that the culprits were her brothers. Though diviners do not on principle divulge the names of those who commit sorcery, Sugathan was quite certain who they were. When asked how he came to this conclusion, he replied that his wife's brothers "should have been the culprits since he could not build the house because of the trouble they gave him." (The deductive process is as follows. Sugathan wants to build a house; his wife's brothers do not allow him to do so; he falls ill; the diviner attributes it to sorcery; he spends all his money to cure himself and is unable to build the house; therefore, his wife's brothers should have been the ones who made him fall ill.)

Sugathan also claimed that sorcery is directly related to his loss of appetite. In his view, sorcery had affected the meal he had eaten after the encounter with the supernatural; the meal had remained undigested and became "dirt" (kunak, a term also used to refer to a corpse, a dead fetus, rubbish, or to human excreta).

The diviner had prescribed that several curing rituals be performed to rid Sugathan of the effects of sorcery. These rites did not effect a permanent cure. Instead, they exhausted most of the cash he had gathered to build his house; he even had to sell some of the building materials to pay for the rites.[20]

The dispute was not settled at the time I left the village. Though Sugathan had appealed to the Conciliation Board for a settlement, he expressed some scepticism about a fair settlement, since he knew that his affines had considerable influence with the Board members. He is still a sick man and complains of a lack of appetite. During the year 1971, he had begun to take an interest in the religious life; in particular, he had begun to make pilgrimages thrice a year to the shrine of a major national deity, called Kataragama (the shrine is situated about 90 miles south of Mulgama). I have indicated how his counterpart in the earlier dispute had adopted a similar orientation.

18 The objective is to control or arrest the illness. Threads of cotton are charmed with magical formulae and then tied around the patient's neck, wrists or waist (see also Wirz 1954 for a comprehensive account).

19 The common belief is that no source of illness (through sorcery, the maleficence of supernaturals or through natural causes) can affect a person so long as the planets are favorable for him.

20 The costs of having the rites performed were about 500 rupees, which included payments for the ritual specialists and their assistants, cost of preparing food for performers, kinsmen and friends, and the cost of obtaining ingredients and utensils for the rites.

Analysis

Two conflicting processes underlie the sequence of events in disputes, namely, litigation or the appeal to an impartial, judicial body such as the District Court, and the commission or suspicion of sorcery which serves as a regulatory mechanism, being that it maintains the traditional system. It will be seen that litigation and sorcery represent two antagonistic notions of the person, and that each produces a different kind of social outcome.

To the extent that the law of the courts regards all persons equal, irrespective of differences in sex or in the statuses they hold in a culturally defined system of meaning, the law upholds a culturally neutral definition of the person, i.e., as an individual in the Western social and legal sense of the term: "We in the west tend to think of the person as an individual – a breathing, thinking (sometimes even rationally), acting entity. The individual is describable in terms of his or her own characteristic traits of physiognomy and personality... the individual, in other words, is describable as an isolate without necessary reference to any other person" (Lieber 1973).

The individual in the Western tradition is the analogue (though not the homologue) of the whole person as an emic category in Sinhalese peasant culture. Thus, when a villager goes before a court of law a remarkable transition takes place, this being, in the terms of F. S. C. Northrop, a change in "the concept of the person and his secular or religious customs from the kinship anthropological to an egalitarian contractual basis in which all individuals... stand equal, existentially consentual, and, therefore, meaningfully self-responsible before a contractual common law" (1968:6).[21]

The court could or would confer what would amount to a whole-person status to an outsider by recognizing equality of claim between males and females, and by partitioning a share of the estate and, thereby, creating a whole estate from a part. However, land is only *one* attribute of the whole person in Mulgama terms; kinship, the sharing of blood and surname of a given ancestor, and citizenship constitute equally important dimensions of the concept of the whole person. In other words, a part person who has converted his share into a whole estate through partition is an anomaly, and litigation is a process leading to an anomalous state in an entire system of meanings.

Villagers are aware of the principles upheld by the courts; this is reflected in the statement made by the citizens in each dispute that if the outsider wishes to have his "due" share, he should go to court. However, litigation is also a costly and time-consuming endeavour which most villagers are unwilling or financially incapable of undertaking. For example, though the law allows for the partition of an estate, partition is an elaborate procedure which requires that the plaintiff provide documentary evidence in support of his claim, that he obtain the co-operation of co-parceners to appear in court and to agree to a partition, and that he be prepared to pay the fees of lawyers, and the costs

21 I am thankful to my friend, Norman Riise, for introducing me to this and several other stimulating works by Northrop.

of obtaining documents to support his claim (e.g., certificates of birth, marriage and death and copies of wills and deeds). Though all co-parceners will share these costs with the plaintiff after partition has taken place, most villagers do not have the resources to suffer these costs initially.

It is often the case that a litigant will either be reduced to a state of poverty or by undertaking litigation he will sacrifice other interests and endeavors. Thus, in Dispute No. 1, the outsider chooses to spend his money on rebuilding his house rather than go to court. His counterpart in Dispute No. 2 appeals to a lower court, the local Conciliation Board which could make a decision in favor of the citizens since the latter have political and kin ties with the members of the Board.

A key process within the village community, namely sorcery, counteracts the attempts of the outsider to use the courts (the outside) to change conditions inside the village. Sorcery stands in a significant relation to the outsider as an individual, as a participant within a system of norms governing rights in land and residence, and as a member of a category of persons within a total conceptual scheme. The relationship of sorcery to the outsider is simply that it nullifies or neutralizes the anomaly that he can become through litigation.

The term for sorcery (*suniyam*, from the root *sunya* meaning "nothing" or "the void") as well as the term for objects used in sorcery (*palua*) are both associated with ideas of waste, disintegration, and desolation. For example, the destruction of a (whole) object by violent force is referred to as *sunu visunu karanava* (verb; *sunu* again a derivative from the root *sunya*, + *visunu* or "thrown" + *karanava* or "to do"). To destroy something is, therefore, to separate the whole into parts, i.e., to disintegrate. The term for objects used in sorcery (*palua*) is associated with the social circumstances within which peasant life takes place. The term denotes (a) the failure of a natural process to achieve completion or fruition, for example, a crop failure due to lack of rain or pests referred to as *vaga palua*; (b) erosion (*hoda palua*) of land by the action of rain whereby the fertile topsoil is removed and a layer of sandy soil or rock is exposed; (c) the eradication of or harm done to crops, for example, by grazing cattle (*idam palua*); (d) wasteland (*palu idam*), a stretch of ground which is uninhabited, desolate or where nothing grows; and, (e) isolation or loneliness experienced by an individual (*palua*). The meanings of waste, discontinuity, loss of fertility and vitality, and isolation are directly antithetical to the meanings associated with kinship and land tenure which emphasize continuity of blood ties, the continued use of land by a group of agnates, the nurturance derived from the use of land and the equation of land use with eating and with food, all of which define the whole (and the wholesome) person.

The relation of sorcery to the system of norms governing kinship, residence and land tenure can be treated in two ways. At the terminological level, there is the equation of illness (*dos*) with the concept of a moral wrong or the violation of a set of shared expectations; i.e., the term *dos* embraces illness stemming from the maleficence of planetary deities, gods, demons, or the spirits of dead kin as well as the infringement of a person's rights, the failure to perform a duty or obligation or an act of discourtesy. In the context of these meanings the attribution of his ills to sorcery is also a symbolic statement made by the outsider that he has violated the moral order by demanding the rights of an insider. The idea is specifically conveyed by the statement of the outsider (in Dispute No. 2) that due to sorcery he has lost his appetite and that what he has eaten remains undigested. Whereas the use of land is equated with ideas of food and nourishment, sorcery contributes to loss of nourishment from what is eaten, and to an inability to eat, i.e., use land.

At a more general level sorcery functions as a regulatory mechanism in a social context where formal institutions for settling disputes are absent or lacking. Once the outsider begins to suspect sorcery he exhausts all his wealth trying to eliminate the effects of sorcery. In so doing he dissipates cash, a crucial resource for manipulating the courts to change his rights in the village.

Sorcery is also a statement about the conceptual status of the individual committing sorcery or suspecting it. Though everyone in the village believes in the efficacy of sorcery, it is the outsider who has a high emotional investment in the phenomenon. To commit sorcery or to believe that one is the victim of sorcery is to acknowledge that there is a separateness or boundary between the victim and the persecutor, that they do not share solidary relations, and that they are not the same category of person.

Conclusion

My focus has been on the conceptual relations which define the person in Sinhalese peasant society. In this conceptual scheme, individuals fall into distinct categories of persons; the system of person classification is made with reference to a set of relations the terms of which are "whole" and "part". Whole and part relations also define the persons in regard to kinship and rights in land. To this extent, it becomes impossible to view events such as land disputes purely as "economic" or "legal" phenomena, since land disputes automatically involve the larger scheme of relations defining the person. By the same token, the peasant is more than a pragmatic materialist, as Leach, for example, makes him out to be. The peasant is also a relational thinker who conceives the material world in symbolic terms.

Perhaps the major source of tension within the culturally defined system of person classification is the prevalence of a tradition of contractual law introduced through foreign rule, for contractual law and the courts which uphold it represent a culturally neutral definition of the person; all individuals are existentially equal before the law. The existence of this legal tradition and the influence it exerts on peasant society in Sri Lanka probably marks a stage of transition from "the law of status" to "the law of contract", to use Maine's evolutionary typology.

At the same time, to the extent that status distinctions in caste, sub-caste, property rights and citizenship in village communities persist in Sri Lanka as well as in South Asia, the transition will necessarily be a slow one. In place of a law before which all persons are existentially equal South Asian society offers the individual the conceptual scheme of its great religions before which all individuals are ultimately status neutrals. The casteless role of the *sannyasi* in Indian society is a classic example, as are the religious inclinations of the two persons ending their secular careers in the disputes.

REFERENCES

GEERTZ, C.
    1966   "Person, Time and Conduct in Bali: An Essay in Cultural Analysis." Yale South-east Asia Program, Cultural Report Series, No. 14.
GUEMPLE, L. (ed.)
    1974   "Kinsman, Person and Actor: Essays in the Culture of Social Relations." Washington, D.C.: American Anthropological Association (Anthropological Studies Series). In press.
LEACH, E. R.
    1968   *Pul Eliya, A Village in Ceylon.* Cambridge: Cambridge University Press. (First edition, 1961.)
LEE, R. W.
    1953   *Introduction to Roman-Dutch Law.* Oxford: Clarendon Press.
LIEBER, M. D.
    1973   "To Be Only a Woman on Kapingamarangi: The Penultimate Insult?" Seattle: unpublished ms.
NORTHROP, F. S. C.
    1968   "Towards a More Comprehensive Concept of the Person" pp. 1–12 in P. T. Raju and A. Castell (eds.), *East-West Studies on the Problem of the Self.* The Hague: Martinus Nijhoff.
SCHNEIDER, D. M.
    1968   *American Kinship: A Cultural Account.* Englewood Cliffs: Prentice-Hall.
SELVADURAI, A. J.
    1973   "Culture and Continuity: A Study of Kinship and Land Tenure in a Sinhalese Village." Seattle: unpublished Ph.D. dissertation.
WIRZ, P.
    1954   *Exorcism and the Art of Healing in Ceylon.* Leiden: E. J. Brill.

Aristocrats and Rituals in Contemporary Ceylon

H. L. SENEVIRATNE

University of Virginia, Charlottesville, U.S.A.

THIS PAPER deals with the use of ritual by the Kandyan aristocrats of Ceylon to express and enhance their political and social status. The rituals, to be briefly described below, are historic, going back at least three centuries. In pre-British times these were rituals of state. After the fall of Kandy to the British in 1815 they were still performed as public rites, the large expenditure involved being paid for by the extensive land grants made to the religious institutions by the Sinhalese kings, and kept relatively intact under the colonial administration.

The Kandyan aristocrats, known as *radala*, are descendants of the Sinhalese chiefs of Kandyan times (c. 1800). They constitute the upper rungs of Goyigama, the highest in the Sinhalese caste system. There is no suggestion here that the present *radala* are direct descendants of the Kandyan chiefs. Most of the Kandyan aristocracy was apparently destroyed during the conflicts with the British.[1] Of those remaining, dwindling fortunes would have undoubtedly driven some out of this group. However, the fact that needs to be remembered for the purposes of this paper is that the present Kandyan aristocracy is believed by itself and in general by the rest of the society to be a continuation of the aristocracy of Kandyan times.

The prevailing rifts between the aristocracy and the bureaucratic elite of modern Ceylon coming largely from the non-Kandyan coastal areas known as the "low country" go back to the early period of British rule in Ceylon. It was part of general British policy in their colonial territories to create an indigenous British-oriented elite to man local administration, a policy well expressed in Macaulay's minute on Indian education urging the need "to form a class of persons Indian in blood and color, but English in tastes, in opinions, in morals and in intellect." In this the British were eminently successful and many facets of later Ceylonese history would be inexplicable without an understanding of this. The instruments of metamorphosis were the schools established largely in the low-country. The result was the exclusion of the

---

1 Lawrie (1898: 203) wrote: "In 1819 hardly a member of the leading families, the heads of the people remained alive; those whom the sword and the gun had spared, cholera and small pox and privations had slain by hundreds."

Kandyan aristocracy from the group of brown-skinned Englishmen envisaged in Macaulay's dictum. It must hastily be added, however, that this does not mean the Kandyan aristocrats remained illiterate in the English language and in foreign manners. Very much to the contrary, they did learn these in the few schools established in Kandy and also by schooling in Colombo. Nor does it mean that no Kandyan aristocrats were employed in administration. What is interesting is that of the Western-educated Kandyan aristocrats only a meager proportion took to administrative employment. This was partly due to their being consciously kept away by distrusting British administrators, fearful of giving power to Kandyan aristocrats who could abuse it. The aristocracy, thus deprived of administrative power which they were traditionally used to, tended to look upon as upstarts the British-created new bureaucratic elite drawn largely from castes traditionally lower than theirs. The bureaucratic elite in its turn, ensconced in power, had no reason to pay deference to the aristocracy and considered its members traditional, pompous and illiterate. From different perspectives, however, the bureaucrats, like the rest of the society, did concede some recognition of the aristocracy as a symbol of a dignified past which the latter seemed to embody in its modes of ceremonial dress, speech and certain aspects of traditional domestic behavior. It is the primary theme of this paper that the Kandyan aristocracy, conscious of this symbolic value of their heritage for the society today has sought to identify themselves with the still surviving traditional rituals of the Kandyan kingdom, and further, to change somewhat the form and content of these rituals in ways suitable for the expression and enhancement of their prestige.

The rituals center around the Sacred Tooth Relic of the Buddha, enshrined in the Temple of the Tooth in Kandy, and the shrines of the four major gods of Ceylon: Natha, Vishnu, Kataragama and Pattini. A central and spectacular part of the ritual is a pageant performed in the lunar month of June–July and known as the *Äsala Perahära*, where the Sacred Tooth Relic and the insignia of the gods are taken in solemn procession through some of the principal streets of the city for ten successive nights. In Kandyan times, the pageant was more than this. Ostensibly a religious pageant for honoring the sacred objects just mentioned, the pageant also expressed in microcosm, among other things, the king's central and provincial administrative machinery. It also accommodated symbols of the king's military might-the elephants department, various departments of artillery, and the regiments. In today's pageant none but the remnants of these remain for the obvious reason that most of the institutions they represented are no longer in existence.

The Kandyan aristocrats, who are the authorities behind the pageant, have replaced these various military formations of the pageant with contingents of dancers who perform the variety of dance known as "Kandyan dance". They have done this for the unusually great public attention the dancers help to confer on themselves when they walk in the pageant. In traditional Kandyan society, the dancer was one of numerous servants who rendered caste service to the lord; the dancers are a caste as are potters, drummers and blacksmiths.

The caste service of the dancer was to entertain the lord and entertainment in this sense was a privilege of the aristocracy. Therefore, to be danced in front of is a sign of high social status. It is in terms of this subtle meaning that the dancer in the pageant, dancing in front of the aristocrat, focuses public attention on him. This is even more so if one recalls that every now and then, the dancers dance particular scores which in the idiom of the Kandyan dance represent the accord of courtly honor to the lord. A glance at the formation of the pageant, which is done at the direction of the aristocrats, shows how underneath the formal objective of honoring the sacred objects, the aristocrats try to steal honor for themselves: in front of the sacred objects in the pageant there are often only a few dancers, but in front of themselves they arrange to have many. Besides the honor the dancers provide in the idiom of the dance and its stylistic conventions, the visual impact of rows of dancers conducting an aristocrat is, to the members of the culture at least, impressive in the extreme. These aristocrats are often active politicians in modern day national or local politics and the pageant is watched by tens of thousands of people who are also voters. In a political system based on popular ballot the benefits of such a display for political contestants need no elaboration. Besides, at strategic points *en route* the leading members of a particular aristocrat's political following would superimpose himself on the pageant and honor his leader by resorting to such acts as decking him in garlands in view of thousands of observers to whom the act would appear spontaneous. Such acts are more frequent during times of national or local elections in which the aristocrats might be contestants. To draw an analogy with America, was it not on the eve of the 1972 elections that President Nixon was seen frequently on television, victoriously toasting to China and the Soviet Union?

The aristocrats make a conscious attempt to identify themselves with the pageant. It is not my intention to deny that by doing so, they are only doing their duty. However, doing a duty does not preclude one from using it for the enhancement, where applicable, of one's prestige. This is precisely what the aristocrats do. Indeed, one may go a step further to suggest that they do their duty when duty and prestige coincide; and, when these do not, they show no great eagerness to perform duties. For example, the aristocrats in general choose to attend and conspicuously play expected roles in rituals which are well known and attended by large numbers of people. When it comes to lesser known and poorly attended rituals, the aristocrats have a tendency to forget their equally obligatory duty to attend and perform ritual roles. Such behavior can be understood only in terms of their political meanings. That is, in identifying themselves with the pageant, the aristocrats are aware of its wide appeal as a symbol of a glorified past and are making a political investment. In the context of Ceylon's present status as a "new" nation emerging from colonial rule this symbolic meaning assumes great importance. It is a common observation in the studies of "new nations" that these nations, in particular during and soon after independence, frequently seek to obtain from its past real or imagined cultural items as fit symbols of the nation's new identity and "resurgence".[2] The Asala pageant is undoubtedly one such symbol and the aristocrats, besides performing their duties which they may well be, are also using the pageant to their own advantage.

The rituals are used by the aristocrats also to express their status in relation to the bureaucratic elite whose historical and sociological origins were briefly discussed earlier. One telling example will illustrate this point. It is the occasion of the official meeting of the aristocrats and bureaucrats for the purpose of discussing public arrangements for the pageant. For the pageant is watched by thousands of people and special arrangements are necessary in matters such as health and sanitation, food and transport. To begin with, the occasion itself is a concession to the status expression of the aristocrats, because in fact the bureaucrats alone end up making these arrangements. But the aristocrats are masters of the ritual and they are in a position to insist that their voices be heard on the matter. The meeting is held at the main government office (*kachcheri*) in Kandy and is presided over by the chief provincial administrator known as the Government Agent. The arrival of the aristocrats at the meeting and the seating habits express the aggressive stance they are soon going to assume. They usually come *en bloc*, and sit on the side of the presiding officer as if in proclamation of status superior to that of the bureaucrats. This contrasts with the manner in which the bureaucrats make their entry: they come casually, and, to all appearances, sit wherever they could find seats or perhaps wherever they reckoned comfortable or expedient, such as under ceiling fans so that they could cool off, or close to a door, so that they could walk off as soon as the meeting was over, if not before. As items such as food, health and transport are taken up in succession, the aristocrats aggressively criticise the proposals of the bureaucrats, usually alleging that their plans on the particular subject failed the previous year. Another way the aristocrats express their status is by their attempt to imply that they are not second in importance to the bureaucrats. They insist that they be given privileges and facilities similar to those of the bureaucrats within the duration of the pageant, on the ground that they perform similar organizational tasks. An interesting request is that which is made for telephones to be connected to the aristocrats' offices within the duration of the pageant. This is not as trivial as it sounds, for in Ceylon there is perhaps no more ubiquitous, bureaucratic accessory, inaudible as it may be, than the telephone.

REFERENCES

GEERTZ, Clifford (ed.)
      1963   *Old Societies and New States*. New York: The Free Press.
LAWRIE, Sir Archibald
      1898   *A Gazateer of the Central Province*. Colombo: The Government Printer.

---

2   See, for example, the following: Singer 1959; Shils 1965; and the essays in Geertz (ed.) 1963.

SHILS, Edward
    1965 *Political Development in the New States.* London: Mouton Press.
SINGER, Milton.
    1959 "Preface" in Milton Singer (ed.); *Traditional India: Structure and Change.* Philadelphia: American Folklore Society.

Monastic and Lay Buddhism in the 1971 Sri Lanka Insurgency

AGEHANANDA BHARATI

University of Syracuse, Syracuse, U.S.A.

I WENT TO Sri Lanka on a grant from the American Institute of Ceylonese Studies to research ideological change and the Buddhist clergy. I settled in the field during the last week of January, 1971. Early March, the U.S. Embassy was attacked, a state of emergency proclaimed, and on April 5 the outbreak happened, as I was driving down an almost deserted road from Nuwara Eliya to Kandy. Contrary to speculations communicated to me that I might have come to the country in order to study insurgency, this was the last thing I had reckoned with – although it was apparent to many Ceylonese that something was going to happen. I saw the signs, not in any metaphorical sense, but painted on the walls at the University in Peradeniya and elsewhere. Being interested in the creation and use of neologisms, the term "*dhaneśvara*" and "*dhanapati*", lit. "lord of wealth," standing for "capitalist" fascinated me, not for its ideological implications, but for the linguistic naivete of the translation, on a par with *madhyasthāne* for "a center".[1] To the ideologically unindoctrinated Sinhalese who knows only Sinhala, "*dhaneśvara*" could not possibly connote what "capitalist" connotes in Western languages. But, by the time this term had become vogue as part of an incipient revolutionary vocabulary in the language, the ideologically disparaging sense of "capitalist" must have been interiorized by the Sinhalese audience for which these terms had been generated.

When the insurgency broke out, the American ambassador suggested that all U.S. citizens voluntarily move into the vicinity of Colombo. An oceanographic vessel belonging to Scripps College in California happened to anchor in port, and the captain was asked by the Embassy to stand by for possible evacuation of U.S. citizens. Upon informing a secretary at the Embassy that I had to return to Kandy where my research interests were focused, I was told that I was on my own. Aren't we all, I replied, and got a polite diplomatic shrug. En route to Kandy, my car was stopped by insurgents near Kegalle, but the young men in their bluish "Guevara" outfits were as polite to me as they

---

1 The term translates as 'center' in an English dictionary, though in the sense of "a point in the middle," not as a point of venue or convocation.

had been to an American colleague's wife whose car they had stopped on her way down from Kandy to Colombo. They had asked her to return to Kandy, which she did, but they let me pass through and made no move to commandeer the taxi in which I was riding. (Other cars had been commandeered; I was just lucky.) The twenty or so year old who must have been the leader of the particular group asked me what I was doing in Sri Lanka. When I said I was studying Buddhism, he and his comrades nodded approvingly and beckoned the driver to move on, which he did at some speed. "There are many Buddhists in America?," he asked after I had told him about my interests. "Yes," I said without lying, since when you put together all Zen Americans and Japanese Americans, the number must be substantial.

Anthropologists usually prepare their research strategy before they go into the field. Though I tend to prefer letting the field generate its own modes of investigation and response, I did have structured enquiry on paper and in my mind. On April 9 I suggested to myself in a note (in German lest somebody should peruse these notes): "No structured enquiry about this situation; first, because that would be dangerous; second, because I did not come to research rebellion; third, because I wouldn't know how to ask direct questions about the insurgency without making myself highly suspicious to say the least." A week later, I had an audience with Mr. Sarat Amanugama, the chief officer in charge of government information. As I was leaving, he said, "I hope you are not going to write a special book about the insurgence." I promised I wouldn't, so I won't. The temptation, of course, was there; to my knowledge, I was the only American cultural anthropologist in the land during the insurgence. (Susan Ripley of the Smithsonian was measuring lemurs and other hominoids in the Anuradhapura district at that time, but her informists were politically quite innocuous.) Whatever notes I did take about the insurgence were spin-offs of my planned enquiries regarding Buddhism and ideological change. To my great delight, I found that laymen and monks volunteered situation-related answers. This, of course, was quite natural. The nation was under grave duress; security was in total jeopardy at least for two weeks; and, people who were not themselves involved in the insurgence were, I thought, more articulate about the situation than they were about ideological matters before the outbreak.

Most importantly for my research, the Buddhist clergy somehow became part of the referential focus in public and private talking and writing about the events. I shall discuss the degree of monastic involvement later, but let me say here that, regardless of whether those I talked to knew or did not know that I was interested in Buddhist monks, the conversation often tilted toward the *sangha* and its members. How much the tilt might ha[ve] unconscious effort on my part to goad the conversation, hidden behind a pillar, sipping tea or something stronger a in Kandy in the first week of May, I overheard a group of were lawyers and one a doctor, speak about the genera involvement of monks came up twice in half an hour. In th legend generated by the course of events, monks seemed invariably to play a part. The newspapers echoed the style: "a woman and a monk were among those arrested."[2] Perhaps the enumeration of definitionally unaggressive types side by side was part of an unplanned dialectic of contrast. In all this, journalists had an easier job than the anthropologist who must, after all, find more instances than just a few to corroborate a thesis. Toward the end of June, when things had more or less calmed down, I obtained an average estimate of monks arrested, of about 300, which if correct would be a high proportion in light of the alleged, gossip-line monkish involvement with the outbreak.

Let me give one strident example. Near Kataragama, I spoke to the mother of Pushpa, a twice-crowned beauty queen of Kataragama and Tissamaharama. The girl was arrested as an insurgent, paraded in the nude by an army officer, then raped, shot and buried in a ditch. Almost everyone I talked with said this girl and a monk were dealt with in similar fashion (except for the rape) and that their bodies shared the same grave. There was no unanimity about this matter, however, among the people most directly affected by the incident, i.e., the family of the girl and the neighbors in houses surrounding the home of the girl's parents. A brother said, "the *hamuduru* got away," and the mother did not seem to know that a monk was a victim alongside her daughter. *'Ä'tte*, the communist Sinhalese language daily, described the whole story in great detail, but no monk was mentioned.

Anthropological field workers know that allegations of situational or of more persistent mischief of an intangible or covert kind are far more frequent than actual occurrence: the best known paradigm, of course, being witchcraft, where accusations exceed, by far, actual witchcraft attempts in most societies. Since no one in any of the more highly affected regions knew how many arrests had been made, nor how many people had actually been involved, they would tend to single out for gossip those individuals who were somehow more interesting in the social system of the areas, people who were culturally defined as nonviolent (*viz.* women, and monks).

In tracing leftist ideology among the Buddhist clergy, a historian of thought would have to take into account many trends remote from the *sangha*. It would not seem that the writings of Marx and Engels, though translated in part into Sinhalese and commented on in many Sinhalese publications going back to the early twenties, have generated a caucus of leftist Buddhist monks. But, if one literary product were to be selected as having had a singularly heavy impact on Buddhist thinking (both monastic and lay), it was *The Revolt in the Temple*,[3] "composed to commemorate 2500 years of the Land, the Race and the Faith," as the subtitle reads. The Sinhalese title, interestingly, was "*dharma-vijaya*", i.e., the victory of the dharma. Though the author uses a pseudonym, everyone knows who he was – a somewhat eccentric sibling brother of a very wealthy man, and a layman. The book is purportedly the first large-scale

---

2 *Ceylon Daily News*, May 14, 1971.
   First published in 1953 in Sinhalese and immediately thereafter in English (Sinha Publications, Colombo 1953).

Marxist interpretation of Buddhist teachings. To the critical reader, it is a rather pompous, historically inaccurate, and naively slanted invective against anything Buddhist *not* ideologically viewed. The work does not project any but the most superficial familiarity with Marxist doctrines; the subtleties of Marxism elude the author who presents a bowdlerized, pamphletistic reading of Marxism. The gist of its 700 pages is easily told. The Buddha was the first harbinger of successful class struggles: the rejection of capitalism, colonialism, and the whole bag of political conservatism is the core of his teachings as well as those of his disciples. The book is out of print (both in Sinhalese and English), though I obtained a copy under the counter from an employee of a large bookshop, who sold me his own copy "at loss" as he told me. I asked a dozen or so monks, senior people, if they knew this book, and all had heard of it. Some ten *samaneras* (novices) of Malvatte and Asgiriya had heard about it, but only two of this whole set said they had actually read the book. And, many young and old *samaneras* and bhikkhus whom I asked denied they had even seen or heard about the book. I will, therefore, not regard this piece as a literary *agent provocateur*, but I do claim that it represents the basic views of a sizeable number of Buddhist clergy (perhaps five per cent of the total monastic population) from over all the Nikāyas. I also think that the instructor who gave the famous five lectures to the would-be insurgents might have read the book as part of the pedagogical training packet. The highschoolish, mnemonic-aphorismic style of those instructions curiously resembles much of the rhetoric in *Revolt in the Temple*. There is, of course, no causal relation between these; rather, they both represent the popular version of what I call "nutshell Buddhism" (after the Ven. Nārada Thera's *Buddhism in a Nutshell*, which is placed atop the Gideon Bible in the better hotels across Sri Lanka). Part of the reform talk in the religious sphere, both in Hindu India and Buddhist Sri Lanka, is precisely this sort of *ad hominem* harangue directed not at illiterates, but a kind of rhetoric meant for school teachers, maybe bank clerks, and what the Indian government refers to as "third division employees".

The difference between normative and actual Buddhism is very great in Theravada countries. When *engagé* Buddhists in Sri Lanka *talk* Buddhism, they usually talk normative Buddhism; not necessarily *dhamma* alone, though this predominates. On the other hand, most Sinhalese do not pretend *not* to worship Kataragama and other gods. Those who do deny the chthonic deities of the land are, quite predictably, the "nutshell" Buddhists and their followers. *The Wheel*, published by the Buddhist Publication Society in Kandy, and the laymen and priests contributing to it either never mention the Ceylonese gods and the local pantheon, or they actually reject this aspect. But I would improve on Gombrich's division between practised and professed Buddhism[4] and would include the Ceylonese pantheon within professed Buddhism, because I regard the "nutshell" Buddhists as deviant. Once non-*dhamma* themes are incorporated

---

4 Cf. *passim* in his *Precept and Practice: Traditional Buddhism in the Rural Highlands of Ceylon* (Oxford: Clarendon Press, 1971).

into normative Sinhalese (or Thai, or Burmese) Buddhism, it could be argued that on that count political action could be normatively justified, so long as some sort of dialectic link to the *dhamma* teachings can be shown. This link can actually be traced without much effort, as many people knowledgeable about Buddhism and interested in showing the link have done. In other words, though no Buddhist would claim that such actions as cataclysmic as self-immolation in Vietnam or taking up arms during the 1971 insurgency conform to specific Buddhist teaching, some texts are quoted which allow, or even recommend social action. The degree of intensity, of course, varies according to the individual interpreter.

This provides the clue to a large segment of radical behavior by Buddhists, though perhaps not of radical Buddhist behavior. A very learned monk near Mt. Lavinia told me that the *Anguttara Nikāya* presents a full set of instructions for public demeanor and social comportment. It has counsel for kings, political leaders, etc.; he quoted passages in Pali which he himself rendered (he did not speak English, but used these terms in English) as the need for "public relations", "discipline", and "punctuality". While high-level vindication of Marxism by quoting the text is rare, even among monks, all apologists for leftist Buddhism *know* that there are texts which do not bar radical interpretation. Once this has been established, there is virtually no limit to politicization of Buddhist doctrine. The lack of specific interdictions in the Tripitaka, and its formalized listing of virtues and demerits (in line with all classical Indian didactic writing), promotes political interpretations of Buddhism – or, for that matter, of any of the Indian religions. One need only mention the pervasive output of Hindu fascist ideas within rightist politics in India today.

From roughly ten of the most learned monks I interviewed – and these were among the most learned monks in the whole land (Belangoda Ānanda Maitreya, Yakkadure Pannatissa, Hemapitigedara Jñānasīha, to mention but three) – I found only two who used their textural erudition to defend, if not *trastavāda* (insurgency), at least strongly socialist or communist ideas. Even these monks did so not because they wanted to justify the actions of the *trastavādis*, nor even perhaps to promulgate socialism, but rather to show that Buddhism was versatile enough to accommodate all these things without recourse to extraneous sources.

"Political Buddhism" means essentially two different things in Sri Lanka, and this difference was polarized in the April–June 1971 insurgency. It means *dhamma* – i.e., oriental, textual literalism as the basis for political action (as in the case of the monastics at Vidyalankara and of such people as the Hemapiti-gedara brothers who got into genuine trouble because of their political Buddhism); or, it means Marxism of varying degrees as foisted on Buddhist doctrine, or, more moderately, the Marxist interpretation of Buddhism, *pace Revolt in the Temple.*

Before I arrived in Sri Lanka, I had supposed there would be some correlations between radical political views and membership in the reformed Nikāyas, and, conversely, between conservative political views and membership in the Siam Nikāya. This initial hunch seemed like common sense and had been fortified by reading Bechert's seminal work[5], plus a long talk I had with him in Goettingen en route to Sri Lanka. My hunch and his highly informed intuition proved quite wrong, however, as there simply is no such correlation either way. In the first place, I found that leftist ideological inclinations among priests and novices depend on several factors which I shall enumerate presently; and, secondly, that there was no systematic tie between Marxist inclinations and sympathy for the *trastavādis*. Although there was a significant correlation between these two, this may not have stemmed from any intrinsic connection between the effect Marxism and the insurgency had on Buddhists, but rather on such trivial coincidences as how close to the *pansala* the *trastavādis* had struck and the tone of editorials in a Sinhalese language daily close to the time of various incidents.

Let me now suggest some factors which contribute, modally speaking, to a Marxist orientation among monks. The most important, though by no means the most obvious, factor is the type of Buddhist exegesis and homiletics a priest or novice has been exposed to, from his *pirivena* or other religious training to the present day. There seems to be an inverse relation between the degree of textual learning, primary source absorption, and attraction to a Marxist stance. In other words, where a monk has studied canonical and commentary Buddhism in traditional detail, his potential interest in popular Marxism tends to be weak; where he has learned Buddhism through simple instructional packets, in Sinhalese rather than in Pali, and in the form of digests rather than through the necessarily bulky primary sources, he is more prone to Marxist ideas, *especially* since these are presented in aphorismic, digested style rather than through Marxist erudition.

I do not know whether any correlation exists between high level Buddhist training and high level (i.e., theoretically, source-oriented Marxist reading), because I met only two learned monks who said they would like to study Marxism in its sources, not the "nutshell" Marxism that Buddhist Marxists know and propound. Martin Wickramasinghe, the famous writer, is probably the most eloquent example of nutshell Buddhism and nutshell Marxism combined. His writings are known to many, if not most, monks. (I encountered his work halfway through my field work, but when I asked questions about it most replies were positive.) One may hazard a guess by analogy to learned Hindu monks: their zest for intensive and extensive handling of religious source material tends to make them interested in imported political ideas; by sheer dint of their training and learning skills, they often sympathize with a doctrine that has generated much discussion, the format of which could be seen as resembling the *śāstrārtha*, i.e., the learned religio-philosophical disputes among the Hindu ideological practitioners. And, of course, in India there have been many well known monastics directly involved in political action, as well as in terrorist

---

5 Heinz Bechert, *Buddhismus, Staat und Gesellschaft in den Ländern des Theravāda-Buddhismus*, Vol. I, II (Frankfurt: Metzner), 1966–1973.

activities (to mention only the early Śri Aurobindo). Dr. Sarathchandra, the renown Sinhalese dramatist and scholar, told me that there was a strong ideological link between the Marxist echelon at Tagore's Visavabharati (Santiniketan) University and some leaders of the Ceylonese left. The entire ashram-like setting of Tagore's institution was bound to generate sympathy among Buddhists who know the importance and the intellectual comfort monastic or paramonastic environments suggest to the Hindu and Buddhist intellectual.

Next in importance to the monk's training, I regard his age. Here, the correlation is more natural and simple: Marxism *and trastavādis* were more acceptable to young monks (i.e., men below forty) than to older ones. However, this did not seem to conform with monastic age in rank; there seemed to be sympathy with the movements about evenly distributed among novices and monks who had had their "higher ordination" (*upasampadā*).

The third factor was obviously the widest one, encompassing several themes: the specific economic situation in which monks find themselves. First, the highly complex problem of monastic estate ownership and transmission of incumbency (see the several articles by Hans-Dieter Evers, a former student of Bechert's, and Bechert's *magnum opus* itself). No incumbents were among those arrested, and I do not know of any incumbent who had been a suspect. But closeness to incumbency as prophylaxis against ideological intrusion of Marxism or of the Janata Vimukti Peramuna type of revolution-now leftism cannot be reckoned as a reliable element; at least a dozen monks who were second-in-charge at *pansalas*, especially in the South (Mutara, Tissamaharama), were among the insurgents. And, I would guess that some imcumbents of poorer estates might have been involved without being detected or arrested. Still, it would seem that monks whose continued solvency was not at stake would not be attracted to the *trastavādis*, although they might conceivably be sympathetic to Marxist doctrine. It is important to remember that the link between Marxism as an ideology and the *trastavādi* outbreak was quite tenuous and totally vague. Those who followed the secular reactions to the events will testify to the great puzzlement and shock displayed by the most articulate leftists in government and politics (of people in power, that is, Mrs. Bandaranaike herself), who in many public addresses lamented the fact that these "misguided youths" were perverting true socialism. "Why are they doing this to us? Why didn't they do it to the previous government?" Political scientists on the Peradeniya campus and at the University in Colombo put it to me like this: To the *trastavādis*, all parties ever in power were exploiters, colonialists; there was no difference between the UNP, the SLFP, and the present coalition. As a result, the insurgents' socialist talk was labelled as mendacious, sheer rhetoric, etc.

When N. M. Perera returned from an official trip to England, his statement about his possible sympathies for the Guevarists was censored by the "competent authority". ("N. M. may say it – the C. A. will censor it," as the somewhat baffling *pukka saheb* commented in his cartoon in the *Ceylon Daily News*). But there is no doubt in my mind that the leftist politicians' fright and disgust with the *trastavādis* was genuine.

It has been pointed out by many that there was a lot of sudden charisma attached to the *trastavādis*, albeit one that defected them after things had calmed down. They were said to be heroic; they were said to have taken vows of extreme, acute austerity – no gambling, no drinking, no smoking, and no sex in spite of the revolutionary co-presence of young women among the insurgents, a co-presence which made them seem much more accessible than in normal village settings. It was this element, actual or fictitious, that drew a good deal of sympathy. A young monk in a small, but well known *vihāraya* in Payingamuwa, near Matale, said this to an audience of half a dozen men and one woman: "What they (the *trastavādi*) do to people is bad; but what they do to themselves is good – they have *sil*; they control themselves; they have the virtues Buddhists are told to create." Courage, singleness of purpose, and the general deferment of pleasures and creaturely comforts in view of a goal were all seen as entirely commendable.

There was a story current in Sri Lanka gossip after thousands of arrested youths had been placed in the detention center on the Vidyodaya campus. "How many Che lectures did you attend?", a man asks a young *détenu*. "Two before the uprising, three in the detention camp," was the answer. The government's naivete in concentrating these people, who had hardly known more than a dozen of each other before the uprising, was in everybody's mouth. One report I heard from several independent sources told of the Venerable Nārada Thera and some other well-known monks being sent into the camp to address the inmates. The priests were booed out, so the story went, and had to leave. Nothing of this made the papers, although those which I read reported that monks had talked to insurgents at the Vidyodaya and other detention centers. There was still time for me to follow up ideas and suggestions germane to this situation. For anthropology's sake, it was irrelevant whether these incidents of rebuff had actually taken place or not. The anthropology of booing is of a subtle kind: if two start this action in a crowd of many, there is likely to be some echoing, regardless of the actual strength of feeling about the mat er or the person booed at. But, it seemed significant that during a period of extreme duress most respondents believed that there had been signs of radical antagonism toward either Buddhist teachings or Buddhist teachers.

In evaluating monastic and lay statement relating to the juxtaposition of Buddhism and Marxism (or any kind of radical leftism), there is usually a simple continuum along which all statements can be aligned: at the most conservative pole, monks and laymen reject any connection between Buddhism and leftist ideology; at the most radical pole, Buddhism itself is rejected. In the center of the continuum, of course, stands the view that true Buddhism is true Marxism, or vice versa, depending upon the ideological starting point of the speaker. Along this continuum, there are about ten variants discernible, based upon different emphases on the spiritual (contemplative, *nirvāna*, etc. elements of the dhamma), or on the social implications of the Buddha's teachings. No one I interviewed tried to square the rule of meditation with anything in leftist ideology; but most people who saw any interconnectedness with socialism apparently believed that the meditational aspects of Buddhism are not its essence, but that the social (anti-caste, active compassion, etc.) elements are.

I now proceed to a very important point, one that is not generally stressed by students of Buddhism, nor by the less involved Buddhists in Sri Lanka. There is a radical difference between the casual, ubiquitous Sri Lanka Buddhist statement amounting to "monks don't really meditate," and what I propose to emphasize as an important part of the etiology of political involvement of the clergy. For it is clear that most Buddhist monks really do *not* meditate; those who do are exceptions, mistrusted often by the hierarchy and their fellow priests in their *pansala*. This includes, of course, the roughly 150 European and American monks on the island, who do nothing but meditate, plus other things that are eminently normative in the Buddhist tradition. There are about a dozen meditation centers (*vipassanā madhyasthāne*, the bizarre neologism mentioned earlier), where monks and laymen engage in contemplation, more or less in strict conformity with instructions laid down in the *suttas* and the *vinaya*. At these centers, the monastic or lay status of the contemplative is irrelevant, though most if not all the teachers are monks. I had the fortune of spending almost a week, due to an unexpected transportational accident connected with the outbreak, with Dr. Ronald D. Laing, the British psychiatrist, who had come to Ceylon to learn Buddhist meditation. He spent close to six weeks at Kanduhodda, one of those meditation centers. The venerable Bhikkhu Sivale, a very serious and senior teacher of Buddhist meditation, later told me that he had never seen anyone, Ceylonese or foreign, monastic or lay, learn meditation as fast as Laing, who would sit up to nine hours a day and three a night. If a monk, either a *sāmanera* or a *bhikkhu*, tried to do this at a *pansala*, he would not last there. This, of course, is not any novel development. Bishop Copleston, not a friendly but a shrewd observer, according to Ven. Ananda Maitreya, wrote in 1892: "As for meditation in any regular form-sitting down for the purpose etc., it is absolutely unknown; 'such things' said one of my informants [i.e., one of Copleston's informants] 'are very non-existent'." He had never heard of anyone even pretending to practice *samādhi*, to use *kammathana*, etc.[6]

This was probably an exaggeration, but it would not appear that the general trend has changed in essence, though the creation of various meditation centers were partly to compensate for this modal lack of normative Buddhist activities among the clergy. Meditation, if done even as a minimal observance, is obviously time-absorbing, leaving little time for secular matters. But the monastics at the *vīharas* follow a fairly circumscribed, hence predictable routine. It includes monastic chores, instructing the laity through formal and

---

6   R. S. Copleston, *Buddhism Primitive and Present in Magadha and Ceylon* (London: Longman Green, 1892), p. 454.

informal sermons and encounters, newspaper reading, and some amount of intramonastic *dhamma* talk. But it does not include meditation. It would appear that no major change in this routine has taken place over the past century, or, if it has, that it would have been in the direction of increased interest in modern, secular pursuits, converging with what the literate laity does in the same locality. Whatever little work is done at the monastery, is done quite regularly, and this includes newspaper reading and talking politics. Averaging ten medium size monasteries (i.e., with more than five and less than fifteen monks) in the Colombo area, two Sinhalese language dailies are bought and read, passing from hand to hand among monks and novices. Though I did not make a count, at least one paper seemed to be read during each week by all the monks of two rural monasteries in the Kandy-Matale area.

I reported earlier that the individual monk's economic distance from the insurgency is a contributing factor in his potential radicalization. Since the poor, Sinhalese-educated village youths made up the majority of the *trastavādis*, it would seem to follow that monks having the same social and economic provenance (i.e., the majority of Ceylonese monks) would be most readily affected by any revolutionary scheme. If unemployment or the sort of employment Mrs. Bandaranaike pointed out most *trastavādis* had at the time of the outbreak (i.e., underemployment in non-ritualistic terms) was a contributing factor among the rural laity, distance from the incumbency and/or poverty of the *pansala* and vīhara would be the monastic equivalent of unemployment and underemployment.

We have now come full circle. To the anthropologist, cross-cultural implications of this episode are more interesting than the episode itself. Sheer professional fascination with the 1971 *trastavādi* situation is the prerogative of historians and political scientists. The anthropologist's concerns are whether this situation either generates or transforms any rules for revolutionary behavior, or whether the event does not follow any pattern at all, resulting from some sort of local idiosyncrasy. An impressive amount of anthropological research and writing has been done on the topic of insurgency. Much of it, unfortunately, has had ominous moorings and potentially counter-operative results – to wit, the infamous Camelot project in Latin America.

In preparing this paper, I checked much of that literature in anthropological journals. The only one I found directly relevant to the Sri Lanka uprising is a recent study by Elliott P. Skinner on political conflict and revolution in an urban area in Upper Volta,[7] the gist of which, or rather the conclusion relevant to our comparative interest being that there are no "viable mediating structures" between the potential or actual rebels and/or revolutionaries and the various governing echelons. Skinner, of course, sees the recent retreat of colonial power as causal for this absence of mediating structures. The tribal system was held together, or better, was prevented from falling apart, due to the presence of an ideologically neutral overriding power. This

---

7 *American Anthropologist* 74/5, October 1972, 1239sq.

part of his analysis is certainly not applicable here; the British had been gone from Ceylon for two decades and a half. Real trouble did not erupt before 1958 (the communal riots), over ten years after the British had left. But there is quite clearly an absence of "viable mediating structures" in the Sri Lanka situation: the bulk of the *trastavādis* were young villagers disenfranchised from political power, devoid of potential and theoretical access to the political and economic power structure. When I say "theoretical", I mean this quite literally: the official claim that every citizen can participate in government (by his ballot, etc.) does not carry operational veracity wherever processes of general participation are established. If a person has only a vote and nothing else, no economic prospects, no job opportunity, etc., then his power through the ballot is of an academic nature so far as he is concerned. The *trastavādis* felt that their voices could not be heard, that they were not heard by the "capitalist" government, and that they were not heard by the present United Front. To add resentment, there was the feeling among them that the Sirimavo government had ridden to power on their backs. Now, of course, promise of participation in power in a situation like that of Sri Lanka is purely ritualistic, and can hardly be anything else, when this promise is directed to the villager. It means something very different, of course, if it is part of a convocation address at Royal or St. Thomas.

Translated into the Sri Lanka situation, Skinner's lack of "viable mediating structures" means simply that there is no intermediary, hence potentially mediating power echelon between the society from which the *trastavādis* recruited themselves and the administrative and political elites in the country. The monks, with the exception of incumbents and their likely successors, fall straight into the very large rural section from which the *trastavādis* emerged. The English-speaking and pamphlet-writing priests of Vajirarama Kelaniya are atypical, by their social origins, for the bulk of monastic personnel. And, if a monk has made good without being an incumbent – by literary or homilectic fame, or by establishing some sort of charisma about his person – then, he dissimulates his humble background or else he flaunts it by implying "see where I come from and look where I now am!". Whatever the actual number of monks and novices arrested, apparently they all belonged to the segments of the rural population which generated the insurgents. And, seen in this light, the wearing of the monastic garb by some insurgents and suspects might be viewed as a rather trivial accident.

INDEX

al-Badr, 69
Allah, Haji Shariat, 76
Amanugama, Sarat, 103
Ambedkar, B. R., 1–5, 8, 9, 13–23
Anguttara Nikāya, 106
Asala Perahara, 98, 100
Asan, Kumaran, 37
Aurobindo, Sri, 108
Awami League, 67, 69–73, 76, 77
Ayyappan, K., 41
Ayyappan, "Sahodaran", 38
Ayyavu, Thykkad, 35

Bandaranaike, Sirimavo (Mrs.), 8, 108, 110, 112
Bangladesh Constitution, 65–68, 70, 73, 76, 79, 80
Bangladesh, First Five-Year Plan (1973–78), 67, 75, 80
Bauls, 74
Bechert, Heinz, 107, 108
Bengal Code, 58
Bengali Academy, 72
Bengali Development Board, 72
Bhutto, Prime Minister, 70
Bira Kishore Deb v. *State of Orissa*, 55
Bombay Hindu Places of Public Worship Act (1956), 61
Bombay Prevention of Excommunication Act (1949), 57
Bombay Public Trusts Act of 1950, 52
British Common Law, 88
British Parliament statutes, 42, 88
Buddhism, 4, 13, 16, 17, 21–23, 29–31, 41, 46, 60, 102, 103, 105–107, 109, 110

Caṇḍī-dās, 74
Castle Disabilities Removal Act of 1850, 58
Chattampi, Swami, 35
Chokha mela, 14, 17, 18, 22
Christians, 22, 25, 26, 39–45, 64, 66, 69, 74
Commissioner, Hindu Religious Endowments, Madras v. *Sirur Mutt*, 51–53, 55
Constituent Assembly (Bangladesh), 65, 66
Copleston, R. S. (Bishop), 110

Dai-ul-Mutlaq, 57–59
Das Gupta, Justice, 59
Davis v. *Benson* (133 U.S. 333 at 342), 51

Dawoodi Bohra Community of Shia Muslims, 57–59
Dharma-nirapekṣatā, 65, 68
Durgah Khawaja Saheb Act of 1955, 60

Engels, F., 104
Evers, Hans-Dieter, 108

Farā'izī Movement, 76, 77

Gajendragadkar, Justice, 54, 60, 61
Gandhi, M. K., 3, 13, 15, 17–19, 33
Gombrich, Richard, 105
Gowda Saraswath Brahman sect, 62
Goyigama, 84, 97

Harijans, 15, 18, 19
Hinduism, 2, 5, 13, 14, 16–19, 21–23, 25, 29, 38, 41, 45, 60, 64
Huq, A. K. Fazlur, 76

Indian Constitution, 3–5, 25, 26, 43, 44, 47–53, 56–63
Indian National Congress, 15, 16, 45
Indian Supreme Court, 50–63
Islam, 16, 21, 42, 60, 67, 68, 71, 78, 80
Izhavas, 1, 3–5, 8, 9, 24–28, 30–46

Jains, 28, 52, 53
Jamā 'at-i Islāmī, 66
Janata Vimukti Peramuna, 108
Jñānasīha, Hemapitigedara, 106

Kabir, 17
Kabir Panth, 17
Kataragama, 98
Krishak Praja Party, 76, 77
Krishnan, C., 37, 41
Kumara Pillai Commission (1964), 45
Kumaran, Murkot, 38
Kumarilabhattan, 28
Kunjuraman, C. V., 38, 41
Kuttan, C., 42

Laing, Ronald D., 110
Lalan Shah, 74
Leach, E. R., 83, 95, 96

Macaulay, T. B., 97, 98

CONTRIBUTORS

Bardwell L. Smith is the John W. Nason Professor of Asian Studies at Carleton College, Northfield, Minnesota. He also served as Dean of the College, 1967–72. He has received his B.A., B.D., M.A., and Ph.D. from Yale University and was a member of the Yale University Council, 1969–74. During 1972–73 he did research at the School of Oriental and African Studies, University of London, on a grant from the American Council of Learned Societies. He has edited a number of books, among them: *The Two Wheels of Dhamma: Essays on the Theravada Tradition in India and Ceylon* (American Academy of Religion, 1972); *Tradition and Change in Theravada Buddhism: Essays on Ceylon and Thailand in the 19th and 20th Centuries* (Leiden: E. J. Brill, 1973); and *Unsui: A Diary of Zen Monastic Life* (Honolulu: University Press of Hawaii, 1973).

Balkrishna Govind Gokhale holds a doctorate from the University of Bombay. He has taught at various colleges and universities, both in India and the United States, and currently holds appointments as a Professor of History and Director of the Asian Studies Program at Wake Forest University, Winston-Salem, North Carolina. Dr. Gokhale is a specialist in Indian history and culture, especially in Pali language and literature, and Theravada Buddhism. He is the author of seven books and numerous articles in leading journals in the U.S., England, Europe, and India. Among his books are: *Indian Thought through the Ages* (Bombay, 1960); *Samudra Gupta, Life and Times* (Bombay, 1962); and *Asoka Maurya* (New York, 1966).

Cyriac K. Pullapilly is Associate Professor of History at St. Mary's College, Notre Dame, Indiana, where he has been since 1970. Prior to that he taught at Middlebury College in Vermont (1967–70) and at the Illinois States University, Normal, Illinois (1965–67). He is a native of Kerala, India, where he did his baccalaureate work at St. Thomas College and St. Joseph's Pontifical Seminary (1948–58). His Ph.D. is from the University of Chicago (1969), with a dissertation on *Caesar Baronius: Counter-Reformation Historian*, which was published in 1974 by the University of Notre Dame Press. He has published several articles in learned journals and is currently completing a book on the St. Thomas Christians of India.

Robert D. Baird is Professor of History of Religions at the University of Iowa, from which university he received his Ph.D. in 1964. He has done field work in India on two occasions: in 1966 as a Postdoctoral Fellow in Asian Religions of the Society for Religion in Higher Education, and in 1972 as a Faculty Fellow of the American Institute of Indian Studies. He is the author of *Category Formation and the History of Religions* (Mouton, 1971); and co-author of *Indian and Far Eastern Religious Traditions* (Harper and Row, 1972). He is also the author of numerous journal articles including "Human Rights Priorities and Indian Religious Thought" (1969) and "Mr. Justice Gajendragadkar and the Religion of the Indian Secular State" (1972).

Joseph T. O'Connell is Assistant Professor of Religious Studies at St. Michael's College in the University of Toronto, where since 1968 (excluding one year for research in Bangladesh) he has taught comparative courses in religion with a concentration upon the Hindu tradition. He has published in the *Journal of the American Oriental Society*, *The Ecumenist*, and *The International Journal*. His research includes a doctoral dissertation on Bengali Vaiṣṇavism and current projects in Bengali Islam, e.g., an anthology of Muslim writings in Bengali and a textual study of the *Satī Maynā o Lor-Candrānī*.

Anthony J. Selvadurai is currently Assistant Professor of Anthropology at San Diego State University in California. He holds a B.A. in English Literature from the University of Sri Lanka, Peradeniya, and an M.A. and Ph.D. (1973) in sociocultural anthropology from the University of Washington, Seattle. The title of his dissertation was "Culture and Continuity: A Study of Kinship and Land Tenure in a Sinhalese Village". His teaching experience has been at the University of Sri Lanka (1971–73), the University of Washington (1973–74), and his present appointment. His primary academic interests include the following: symbolic anthrophology; and the study of the impact of contractual law on South Asian society, and on political and economic change in South Asia.

H. L. Seneviratne is Assistant Professor of Anthropology at the University of Virginia, Charlottesville. He holds a B.A. in Sociology from the University of Sri Lanka, Peradeniya, and an M.A. and Ph.D. (1972) from the University of Rochester in Anthropology. Besides his current position he has also taught at the University of Sri Lanka. He has published several articles on religion and society in Ceylon and his doctoral research was on Kandyan ritual. His primary academic interests are religion and society, sociological theory, politics, and economic development. He has recently taught a course on the sociology of Theravada Buddhism.

Agehananda Bharati is a native of Vienna, Austria and a United States citizen. At Vienna he studied Indology and ethnology and became a monk in the Hindu Dashanami order in 1951. He has taught philosophy at Benares Hindu University, at the Royal Buddhist Academy in Bangkok, and was a visiting professor at both Tokyo University and Kyoto University. From 1961 to 1964 he taught at the Far Eastern Institute at the University of Washington and since 1964 he has been at the University of Syracuse, where he is now professor and Chairman of the Department of Anthropology. Among his numerous publications the following books are important: *The Ochre Robe* (New York: Anchor Doubleday, 1970); *The Tantric Tradition* (New York: Anchor Doubleday, 1970); *The Asians in East Africa: Jayhind and Uhuru* (Chicago, 1972); and *A Functional Analysis of Indian Thought and Its Social Margins* (Benaras, 1964).

UNIVERSITY LIBRARY NOTTINGHAM